T0361648

THE SHORTEST HISTORY OF FRANCE

From Roman Gaul to Revolution
and Cultural Radiance—A Global
Story for Our Times

COLIN JONES

THE EXPERIMENT

NEW YORK

THE SHORTEST HISTORY OF FRANCE: *From Roman Gaul to Revolution and Cultural Radiance—A Global Story for Our Times*
Copyright © 2025 by Colin Jones
Maps and infographics copyright © 2025 by James Nunn
Pages 270–73 are a continuation of this copyright page.

Originally published in the UK by Old Street Publishing. First published in North America in revised form by The Experiment, LLC.

The Experiment, LLC
220 East 23rd Street, Suite 600
New York, NY 10010-4658
theexperimentpublishing.com

THE EXPERIMENT and its colophon are registered trademarks of The Experiment, LLC. Many of the designations used by manufacturers and sellers to distinguish their products are claimed as trademarks. Where those designations appear in this book and The Experiment was aware of a trademark claim, the designations have been capitalized.

The Experiment's books are available at special discounts when purchased in bulk for premiums and sales promotions as well as for fund-raising or educational use. For details, contact us at info@theexperimentpublishing.com.

Library of Congress Cataloging-in-Publication Data

Names: Jones, Colin, 1947- author.
Title: The shortest history of France, from Roman Gaul to revolution and cultural radiance : a global story for our times / Colin Jones.
Description: New York : The Experiment, [2025] | Series: The shortest history series | Includes bibliographical references and index.
Identifiers: LCCN 2024056481 (print) | LCCN 2024056482 (ebook) | ISBN 9798893030129 (paperback) | ISBN 9798893030136 (ebook)
Subjects: LCSH: France--History.
Classification: LCC DC17 .J586 2025 (print) | LCC DC17 (ebook) | DDC 944--dc23/eng/20241129
LC record available at https://lccn.loc.gov/2024056481
LC ebook record available at https://lccn.loc.gov/2024056482

ISBN 979-8-89303-012-9
Ebook ISBN 979-8-89303-013-6

Cover design by Jack Dunnington
Text design by Beth Bugler

Manufactured in the United States of America

First printing March 2025
10 9 8 7 6 5 4 3 2 1

SELECTED ACCLAIM FOR COLIN JONES

On *The Shortest History of France*

"Colin Jones is not only one of the greatest living historians of France, but a terrific writer who has distilled a remarkable quantity of learning, insight, and wit into this concise and wonderfully readable volume. There is no better starting point for readers interested in the history of France and its overseas empires."—**David A. Bell, author of *Napoleon* and Sidney and Ruth Lapidus Professor in the Era of North Atlantic Revolutions, Princeton University**

"Colin Jones has proven that 'shortest' can rhyme with 'best.' Anyone curious about France's long and remarkable history should grab this book. Its style is clear, down-to-earth, and totally absorbing." —**Don and Petie Kladstrup, authors of *Wine and War***

"Moving at the speed of a TGV, and drawing on his deep knowledge of France and its past, Jones deploys his writing talent to show how the history of 'the Hexagon' has always been intimately connected to developments in other parts of Europe and the world." —**Jeremy D. Popkin, author of *A New World Begins* and William T. Bryan Chair of History (emeritus), University of Kentucky**

On *The Fall of Robespierre*

"Vital, incisive, revelatory—takes us to the place, to the instant, to the heartbeat of revolution in the making."—**Hilary Mantel**

"Brilliant. . . . Jones has a marvellous eye for color." —**Dominic Sandbrook, *The Sunday Times***

"Enthralling, incisively argued. . . . a thrilling moment-by-moment examination."—*Financial Times*

On *The Smile Revolution in Eighteenth-Century Paris*

"A compelling Cheshire cat of a book."—*The Guardian*

"The most original approach to history in years. . . one of the most absorbing and unusual history books imaginable."—*The Sunday Times*

"Highly readable, intelligent, unpretentious and even mischievous." —*Times Literary Supplement*

*For Violet (Lettie), Charley,
Thea, and Josh, the "shortest"
of our grandchildren*

CONTENTS

French History: A Timeline

c. 500 BCE Celts settle throughout Gaul

c. 200 BCE–150 CE Roman Warm Period

58–51 BCE Conquest by Julius Caesar

52 BCE Julius Caesar defeats the Gauls under Vercingetorix at battle of Alésia

Late 2nd century CE Beginning of "barbarian" attacks and invasions

451 Defeat of Attila the Hun at the Catalaunian Plains

476 End of the Western Roman Empire

486 Frankish leader Clovis defeats Roman general Syagrius; Frankish expansion begins

496 Clovis baptized and anointed king of the Franks; first ruler of Merovingian dynasty (496–751)

508 Clovis chooses Paris as Frankish capital

511 Death of Clovis and subdivision of kingdom among his sons

c. 530–660 Late Antique Little Ice Age

732 Battle of Tours (or Poitiers): Charles Martel defeats Saracen army

751 Pepin III crowned first ruler of Carolingian dynasty (751–987)

771–814 Reign of Charlemagne; Carolingian cultural renaissance

800 Charlemagne crowned emperor in Rome

842 Strasbourg Oaths: French and German languages begin to diverge

843 Treaty of Verdun: tripartite division of Frankish lands

Late 8th–9th centuries Viking raids and invasions

c. 950–c. 1250 Medieval Warm Period

987 Hugh Capet made king of the West Franks; first monarch of Capetian dynasty (987–1328)

1066 Duke William of Normandy invades and becomes king of England

1095 Pope Innocent III calls for first Crusade

1159–1299 (First) Hundred Years' War against England. Angevin empire extends across western and southern France

1209–1229 Albigensian crusade

1214 Philip II (Philip Augustus) wins significant victory at Battle of Bouvines

c. 1250 Establishment of the Sorbonne

1302 First meeting of the Estates General

1328 Death of last Capetian king, Charles IV; Philip VI founds Valois dynasty (1328–1589)

1337–1453 (Second) Hundred Years' War

1338–1352 Black Death

c. 1350–c. 1850 Little Ice Age

1358 *Jacquerie* (peasant revolt) in northern France

1360 Treaty of Brétigny and English dominance of France

1394 Expulsion of Jews

1415 English victory at Battle of Agincourt

1421–1436 France under English rule

1429 Siege of Orléans raised by Joan of Arc

1431 Joan of Arc burned at the stake

1439 Estates General grants kings right to levy a national tax (the *taille*) to pay for a standing army

c. 1450 Print revolution begins

1453 Battle of Castillon: end of Hundred Years' War

1477 Death of Charles the Bold, duke of Burgundy

1492 Christopher Columbus lands in the Americas

1494 Charles VIII leads expedition into Italy; start of Italian Wars (1494–1559)

1517 Martin Luther posts 95 Theses; beginning of Reformation

1525 Battle of Pavia: King Francis I taken prisoner

c. 1530 Jean Calvin establishes Calvinist branch of Protestantism

1539 Edict of Villers-Cotterêts: French becomes language of law and administration

1559 Treaty of Cateau-Cambrésis ends the Italian Wars

1561–1598 Wars of Religion

1572 Saint Bartholomew's Massacre

1589 Henry of Navarre accedes to the throne as Henry IV, the first of the Bourbon dynasty (1589–1792, 1814–1830)

1598 Edict of Nantes: toleration for Protestants

c.1600 Beginnings of Counter-Reformation in France

1610 Assassination of Henry IV, accession of Louis XIII

1618–1648 Thirty Years' War

1624–1642 Cardinal Richelieu chief minister of King Louis XIII

1631 Creation of the *Gazette*, the first national newspaper

1635 Foundation of the *Académie française*

1638 Birth of Louis XIV, accedes to throne with Marie de' Medici as regent

1642–1661 Cardinal Mazarin chief minister under Louis XIII and Louis XIV

1648–1652 The Fronde (civil wars)

1682 Louis XIV establishes royal court and government at Versailles

1685 Revocation of the Edict of Nantes; introduction of *Code noir* for the colonies

1701–1713 War of Spanish Succession

1715 Death of Louis XIV, regency of the duke of Orléans

1723 Louis XV accedes to throne

1751–1772 Publication of the *Encyclopédie*, the "Enlightenment Bible"

1756–1763 Seven Years' War

1774 Death of Louis XV, accession of Louis XVI

1778–1783 French involvement in the American War of Independence

1789 Fall of Bastille, start of French Revolution; Declaration of the Rights of Man

1791 Slave revolt in Saint-Domingue

1792–1815 French Revolution and Revolutionary Wars

1792 Overthrow of the monarchy, First Republic founded

1793 Execution of Louis XVI

1793–1794 The Terror

1795–1799 The Directory

1798 Napoleon's Egyptian campaign

1799 Coup d'état by Napoleon, overthrow of Directory and establishment of Consulate

1804 Napoleon becomes emperor, end of First Republic; Haiti (formerly Saint-Domingue) declares independence

1808–1814 Spanish Peninsula War

1812 Moscow campaign

1814 Overthrow of Napoleon; Bourbon restoration under Louis XVIII

1815 Napoleon escapes; the Hundred Days, battle of Waterloo, exile; Congress of Vienna

1830 Invasion of Algeria; the *Trois Glorieuses* revolt: end of the Bourbon regime, establishment of the July Monarchy under King Louis-Philippe

1832 Cholera epidemic

1848 Revolution, end of July Monarchy, establishment of Second Republic; abolition of slavery

1852 End of Second Republic. Louis Bonaparte becomes Emperor Napoleon III

1852–1870 Urban renewal of Paris under Haussmann, Prefect of Paris

1863 Victor Hugo, *Les Misérables*

1870 Franco-Prussian War; loss of Alsace and Lorraine to Germany; Second Empire replaced by Third Republic

1871 The Paris Commune

1881–1882 Jules Ferry's primary education reforms

1889, 1900 Universal Expositions in Paris; Eiffel Tower erected

1894–1906 Dreyfus Affair

1905 Formal separation of church and state

1914–1918 First World War

1916 Battle of Verdun

1919 Versailles peace treaties; restoration of Alsace and Lorraine

1934 Stavisky Affair

1936 Left-wing Popular Front: Matignon Agreements guarantee workers' rights

1939–1945 Second World War

1940 German Blitzkrieg; Fall of France; end of Third Republic

1900–1944 *l'État français* or Vichy regime

1944 D-Day landings; liberation of Paris

1945–1946 End of war; provisional government under Charles de Gaulle; establishment of Fourth Republic

1945–1976 The *Trente Glorieuses*, record economic growth

1951 European Coal and Steel Community, precursor to the European Union

1954 Defeat at Dien Bien Phu in Vietnam

1954–1962 Algerian War

1957 Treaty of Rome, creation of Common Market

1958 Political and constitutional crisis over Algeria; end of Fourth Republic, foundation of Fifth Republic with de Gaulle as President

1960 Major decolonization agreements

1962 Treaty of Évian: end of Algerian war, creation of an independent Algeria

1968 "May Events," Grenelle Agreements

1971 Marcel Ophuls, *Le Chagrin et la pitié*

1981–1995 Socialist François Mitterrand longest-serving president

1989 The *foulard* (headscarf) affair

1992 Maastricht Treaty: formation of European Union

1995–2007 Jacques Chirac president

1998 Sentencing in Papon Affair; France wins soccer World Cup

2000 *Parité* law on female representation

2002 Chirac wins second term as president, defeating Jean-Marie Le Pen (National Front) in run-off

2005 Nationwide riots

2007–2012 Nicolas Sarkozy president

2008 International banking crisis

2012–2017 Socialist François Hollande president

2015 Terrorist attacks: *Charlie Hebdo* and Bataclan; Paris Climate Accords

2017 Election of Emmanuel Macron as president

2018 *Gilets jaunes* demonstrations

2019 Fire at Notre-Dame cathedral

2020–2021 COVID-19 pandemic

2022 Macron reelected president

2022 Ukraine invaded by Russia: French aid to Ukraine

2023 Pension law reform and nationwide demonstrations

2024 Legislative elections; Olympic Games

INTRODUCTION
The Hexagon

> No country is the exclusive artisan of its own civilization.
> Paul Vidal de La Blache (1903)

Visiting France as a teenager, I remember being struck by the small, roughly hexagonal plastic templates of the country that were available in stationery shops among the school supplies. Their aim, I suppose, was to familiarize primary school children with the outline and geography of *l'Hexagone*, as many French people refer to their country.

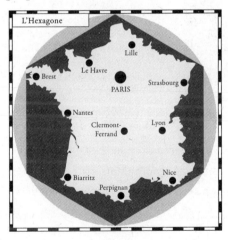

L'Hexagone

Lille
Le Havre
Brest
PARIS
Strasbourg
Nantes
Clermont-Ferrand
Lyon
Biarritz
Nice
Perpignan

The idea of France as a hexagon was popularized in the mid-nineteenth century, the golden age of French nationalism, when the country's modern political contours were being firmed up.

An English friend who spent her early schooldays in France tells me these six-sided templates, still widely available today, led her to believe the country was an island. Regrettably, many writers still give the impression that France and its history have been made solely within these sharply defined "hexagonal" borders.

This book offers something different. While telling the story of the nation and its culture from within, it also shows the extent to which France has been shaped by events and developments well beyond its frontiers.* Unlike the hard edges of those little plastic hexagons, French borders have always been porous. In the globalized world of the twenty-first century, we are used to the notion that flows of people, goods, ideas, and even viruses transcend national boundaries. Yet none of these developments is new. France has never been an impregnable fortress.

"How French!" A woman on a tricycle delivers bread in Paris c. 1901. In 2022, the baguette entered UNESCO's inventory of the world's intangible cultural heritage. In fact, this quintessentially French food was invented in 1837 by an Austrian-born baker, August Zang, albeit in a Parisian bakery.

France has profoundly influenced the course of global history, notably through trade, conquest, and colonization. And while English may be the *lingua franca* of today's globalized world, the French language remains a significant tool of the country's soft

---

*In this it takes its cue from some leading French historians. See especially Patrick Boucheron, *France in the World: A New Global History* (2021), which contains contributions from over a hundred historians, as well as the brilliant pioneering work of Lucien Febvre and François Crouzet, *Nous sommes des sang-mêlés: Manuel d'histoire de la civilization française*. Written in the early 1950s, the latter was only published in 2012 and has not been translated into English. A general bibliography in English is provided at the end of this book.

power abroad. More subtly, too, French art, architecture, music, and literature continue to have a global reach, to say nothing of the democratic political ideals of the French Revolution.

From the very earliest times, France has received as much as it has given. Archaeological and DNA evidence suggest that this area of Europe experienced three prehistoric waves of settlement following the great migrations of *Homo sapiens* out of Africa. The first was around fifty-five thousand years ago, when groups of hunter-gatherers encountered and ultimately replaced Neanderthal

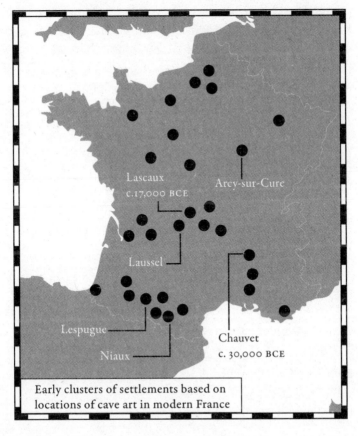

Early clusters of settlements based on locations of cave art in modern France

populations already living in the region. Their descendants would go on to create the extraordinary cave-paintings discovered at Lascaux and Chauvet.

Some time after 7000 BCE, a second wave of settlers, farmers from Anatolia in present-day Turkey, migrated across the continent, largely eradicating existing hunter-gathering populations as they went. Between 5,000 and 4,800 years ago, nomadic herding cultures swept in from the east. They had emerged from the Pontic-Caspian steppe—an area that extends from present-day Bulgaria to Kazakhstan—and may have been fleeing climatic changes, famine, disease, or some combination of all three. They brought with them a Bronze Age culture and probably the Indo-European language as well. Many of these warrior bands interbred with local women, settling down and becoming farmers.

It is thus worth bearing in mind that even the most "indigenous" French men and women are genetic hybrids, bearing a mélange of DNA from across the globe. Some of the earliest inhabitants of France had dark skin and blue eyes, while later arrivals had olive complexions and dark hair. Immigrants with paler skin would come later still. Over the past two millennia, French genetic stock has continued to be shaped by the inward migration of Italian, Germanic, Nordic, and Eurasian newcomers, as well as more recent post-colonial arrivals from Africa, the Caribbean, East Asia, and beyond. As a melting pot of chromosomes and cultures, France bears comparison with—and by some measures surpasses—the United States.

Today the ethnic diversity of France is evident from a quick glance around any Paris subway car. But many famous French men and women of the past had foreign origins too. France's first king (Clovis) and emperor (Charlemagne) were Germans.

Had he been born only a year earlier, before the island of Corsica became part of France, Napoleon would have been Genoese. The Paris Panthéon that honors France's greatest men and women contains the remains of the scientist Marie Curie, who was Polish, and Alexandre Dumas, whose grandmother was a Caribbean slave. No fewer than six of the ten francophone winners of the Nobel Prize for Literature since 1945 have "non-hexagonal" roots. Meanwhile, the film director Jean-Luc Godard was Swiss, the *chansonnier* Charles Aznavour Armenian, and "the French Elvis" Johnny Hallyday half Belgian, while the singer-songwriter Aya Nakamura is half Malian. And so on. The French firmament is and always has been crowded with foreign stars.

The same goes for much of France's most cherished cultural patrimony. Gothic architecture took inspiration from the Islamic world, while many Loire châteaux are copycat versions of Italian Renaissance *palazzi*. "Typically" French public parks were originally modeled on Italian formal styles or else on English landscape

Les Pains de Picasso by Robert Doisneau, 1959: Catalonian by birth, Picasso spent much of his life in France.

gardens. Many of the trees that line their promenades and city boulevards—chestnut, lime, cypress, and eucalyptus, as well as Monet's beloved poplars—are imports, some quite recent.

The national dish *biftek et frites* takes half its name from English, while potatoes come from the Americas. The classic French breakfast of *café au lait* and croissants is a similarly global medley: croissants are styled after Austrian pastries, coffee first arrived in France from Turkey and later came (along with sugar) from the Caribbean, while most of France's dairy products are created with the milk of Holstein Friesian cows.

As this small selection shows, France has never been an empty vessel into which the world has poured its wares. It has reshaped ideas, commodities, and forms of behavior in its own manner, often re-exporting them as "quintessentially French" products.

There is a well-known proverb, "It takes a village to raise a child." Any person's successes, however great, are grounded in the achievements of the wider community. The same principle applies to a nation-state such as France, which has been shaped not only by the efforts and imaginations of countless French men and women but also by innumerable influences from the global community. At a time when nativist, xenophobic, and white supremacist messages are being openly deployed by populist politicians—in France as well as other countries—this is an important message for a national history of the Hexagon to convey.

CHAPTER 1

ON ROMAN COATTAILS

The First Millennium (52 BCE–1000 CE)

Vercingetorix the nationalist hero, as seen in 1865: The plinth reads, "Gaul united, forming a single nation and animated by the same spirit, could defy the universe."

Alésia: A Glorious Defeat

From a towering twenty-three-foot-high structure on Mont Auxois, near the modern spa town of Alise-Sainte-Reine in Burgundy, a huge bronze statue of the Gaulish warlord Vercingetorix looks down somberly on the site of the battle of Alésia. Here in 52 BCE, the forces under his command were routed by the Roman generalissimo Julius Caesar.

Alésia is a good place to start a history of France. It marks the moment when written records appear for the first time in a hitherto wholly oral culture. While the battle was a defeat, it was a glorious one that linked French destiny to classical civilization. Until the nineteenth century, the story of France had traditionally begun in 496 CE with the coronation of Clovis, the Frankish ruler deemed France's first king. But this convention rankled the anti-monarchist and republican historians of the period. The Clovis story also felt a little too German at a time of rising French nationalism. Instead, every schoolchild across the French-speaking empire was taught to admire Vercinge- torix as a proto-nationalist and resistance fighter. Young citizens from the Île-de-France to Indochina were encouraged to revere "their" Gaulish ancestors—*nos ancêtres les Gaulois*—whose fiery blood was held to run through the veins of modern French men and women.

Yet the Vercingetorix myth is largely based on wishful thinking. The little we know of the tribal chieftain mostly comes from Julius Caesar's account of his triumph in *The Gallic Wars*, and the future Roman emperor had every reason to beef up his opponent in order to burnish his own military reputation. The bronze Vercingetorix of 1865 wears anachronistic clothes, bears an outdated Bronze Age sword, and sports a florid mustache that is based on the sheerest guesswork: coins discovered at Alésia show him clean-shaven. It is a representation of Gaulishness that is as much a reflection of its age as Asterix is of our own.

Asterix the Gaul

"The year is 50 BC. Gaul is entirely occupied by the Romans. Well, not entirely. One small village of indom- itable Gauls still holds out against the invaders." With these opening words, the authors of the hugely popular Asterix books offer a comic antidote to Caesar's *Gallic Wars*. Since their first appearance in 1959, the adventures of the diminutive resistance hero and his faithful com- panion Obelix have stretched to over forty volumes, with world sales approaching four hundred million. The Asterix brand is used to advertize everything from washing powder to climbing boots and false mustaches, while Parc Astérix is one of France's most-visited theme parks. Most French men and women have read at least one adventure in the series—and not only as children, since the comic-book (*bande dessinée*) genre is popular among adults too. The humor of Asterix is aimed at all ages, with storylines, references, and visual gags that affectionately lampoon stereotypes from French history.

This icon of modern French culture was invented by the storyteller René Goscinny, a Polish Jew born in France who spent his childhood in Argentina, and the artist Albert Uderzo, the child of Italian immigrants. Scratch a French icon and traces of the wider world are never far beneath the surface.

Any hunt for premonitions of future national glory in Roman Gaul would be futile, however. The area that eventually became France was in constant flux in the centuries after the battle of Alésia, as Italian, Germanic, Arab, Magyar, Scandinavian, and many other outsiders made their mark. Two of these groups imposed their rule directly: first, until the fifth century, the great global Roman empire; then a string of Germanic kings and emperors whose origins and power base lay to the east. Even when it was not under external control, the future Hexagon was fracturing internally and splintering into smaller groupings. Frontiers? There were no stable frontiers.

The Invention of Gaul

France trailed into history on Roman coattails. "Gaul" and "the Gauls" were Julius Caesar's invention: the warriors he defeated at Alésia were Celts. Settling in the Hexagon from around 500 BCE, they formed part of a sprawling agglomeration of peoples that stretched well beyond the frontiers of present-day France, from the Atlantic in the west to the Danube and beyond into Asia Minor. The Celts shared not only similar farming and herding lifestyles but also a common culture and language, at least up to a point—Vercingetorix would have struggled to understand a Gael or a Galatian.

The Romans made "Gaul" a political reality, organizing the area they had conquered into a group of colonies that bore little resemblance to pre-existing arrangements. Pre-conquest Gaul—like the rest of the Celtic world—was a tangle of tribal groupings and settlements, each ruled by a warrior elite. After Alésia, the Romans organized these sixty or so "peoples" into three provinces, collectively and unflatteringly known as *Gallia comata* or "Hairy Gaul."

Gaul: Three Parts or Four?

Gallia est omnis divisa in partes tres. Caesar's lofty opening to *The Gallic Wars* laid out the three divisions of his spoils, covering an area that extended into what is

now Switzerland, Germany, and the Low Countries. Yet he omitted the Mediterranean coastal strip of Gallia Narbonensis, under Roman control since 121 BCE. This zone had long been home to Phoenician,

Etruscan and other merchants—a Greek colony was founded at Marseille in about 600 BCE. It also proved to be Gaul's most Romanized region, containing many of its biggest cities and monuments. At the local level, former Celtic groupings were reorganized as *civitates*, communities centered around a principal town or stronghold.

Caesar regarded the Celtic peoples beyond Gaul's eastern frontier as quite distinct. He gave them a new name too: *Germani*. According to his account, the Germans were pastoralists, rather than settled farmers, who did not follow the druidic form of worship current among the Gauls. Above all, they were more warlike than their neighbors. Caesar defeated these hotheaded tribes in brutal military campaigns in 58 and 55 BCE but never brought them fully under Roman control. Instead, he erected a fortified defensive system along the Rhine (and later the Danube). The *limes*, as it came to be known, was designed to keep the Germans out of Gaul.

Hairy but Loyal: Gaul under the Romans

Meanwhile, Rome imposed its will on the Gauls with an iron fist. The *Pax Romana* came at a cost. The wars that climaxed at Alésia were brutal, with entire civilian populations massacred or kept as slaves after their defeat in battle. Perhaps a million Gauls died and a further million were enslaved out of a pre-conquest total of six to eight million. Vercingetorix himself was humiliated: dragged to Rome in 46 BCE and paraded in the official triumph celebrating Caesar's victories before being garrotted in his prison cell.

Once they had been subdued, the Gauls were controlled with a relatively light touch. Rome expected docility and obedience, payment of taxes, acceptance of military service, and adoption of the Latin language. Mostly, it got what it wanted. The heaviest concentrations of troops were stationed near the Rhine to keep an eye on the Germans. By contrast, Gaulish resistance was sparse and scattered (Asterix notwithstanding). There were occasional rumblings in the countryside, yet the local elite soon grasped the advantages of collusion, and Roman Gaul was largely governed by Gauls working for the Romans. In 48 CE, the emperor Claudius publicly complimented his hirsute subjects on their embrace of the Pax Romana.

> I openly plead the cause of "Hairy Gaul." I would set one hundred years of unbridled loyalty and devotion in a great many difficult circumstances against the objection that they fought the divine Julius for ten years.

Admirers often talk of a unified "Gallo-Roman" culture, but in reality Gaul was anything but homogeneous, while any implied equality between conqueror and conquered is sheer fantasy. The Gauls were always juniors in a partnership that testified to the shrewd Roman strategy of co-opting the defeated. In the immediate aftermath of Caesar's victory, the Romans offered citizenship to local magistrates. In 212 CE the offer was extended to free men throughout the wider empire. These inclusive gestures helped to forge a pliant urban elite, eager to climb the social ladder and occupy administrative and even military positions. Some Gaulish words and place names survived, but by the sixth century Latin monikers had largely replaced local Celtic ones.

The Gauls effortlessly adopted the cult of the emperor and of the Roman gods, which they grafted onto their existing polytheistic

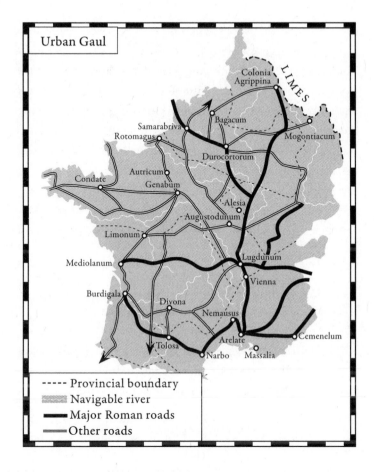

Urban Gaul

- - - - Provincial boundary
Navigable river
Major Roman roads
Other roads

beliefs. Constantine's decision in 313 to extend toleration to the empire's Christians also helped the acculturation process. Christianity had been introduced to Gaul by Asian, African, and German missionaries and at first was a source of conflict. But its later adoption as the Roman state religion helped it eliminate rival faiths. In Gaul, the role of the papacy in Rome was strengthened by the fact that its religious dioceses assumed the same boundaries as secular *civitates*, with bishops playing significant roles in local government alongside lay magistrates.

Better roads were a common good. If the raison d'être of the Roman road network was to mobilize troops swiftly into any area of tension in Gaul and other parts of the empire, it also boosted the economy, supplementing long-distance, sea-based trading. Older cities in the south such as Marseille (*Massalia*) benefited most from the Roman *imperium*, being close to dynamic Mediterranean trade routes. Merchant communities of Greeks, Syrians, and Jews lubricated the Gaulish wheels of commerce—literally so, as the Gauls acquired a reputation for an immoderate love of wine.

> The Gauls are exceedingly addicted to the use of wine and fill themselves with wine brought into their country by merchants, drinking it unmixed, and since they partake of it without moderation by reason of their craving for it, when they are drunk they fall into a stupor or a state of madness. . . . In exchange for an amphora of wine the merchants receive a slave.
>
> Diodorus Siculus (first century BCE)

Vine cultivation diversified an economy based on cereal production and livestock farming. In the south, luxury villa estates were built and worked by slave laborers, producing olive oil, wine, fruit, and grain not only for the domestic market but also the wider empire. The relatively stable, warm, and wet conditions of the Roman Warm Period (from about 200 BCE to around 150 CE) helped to keep crop yields high.

Bread, Baths, and Beyond

In the cities, the local elite were well fed and lived Roman high life to the full. Gaulish cities boasted as many as eighty theaters between them and nearly as many other entertainment venues such as circuses. These were con-

tained within the familiar Roman urban grid system, along-side the forum, baths, temples, curia, and other civic buildings.

The Roman amphitheater at Arles

Decline, Fall, and Global Winter

At its height, the Roman empire was a global power, spanning three continents and stretching from Scotland to the Sahara and from the Atlantic to Mesopotamia. It seemed to have been built to last. It didn't.

Major climatic, demographic, and environmental changes eventually proved too much for Roman Gaul, and indeed for the whole empire. As the Roman Warm Period came to an end, the prosperity it helped to foster began to erode. First the climate became less predictable. Then, after about 450 CE, it turned plain bad as the Late Antique Little Ice Age kicked in. Severe global volcanic activity in the mid-sixth century had a powerful cooling effect, piling on the environmental agony.

Climate Change in Europe

France has endured several notable climatic changes in the past, though human activity has only been a major factor in the modern era. The most significant periods* are referred to here using the following terms.

Roman Warm Period	200 BCE–150 CE
Late Antique Little Ice Age	530–660
Medieval Warm Period	950–1250
Little Ice Age	1350–1850
Global Warming	1850–present

All dates are approximate.

A succession of pandemics ripped through the social fabric of the Roman empire. Its trading links with far-flung places in China, India, and Africa made it especially vulnerable to the importing of new diseases. The so-called Antonine Plague (165–80)—probably an early form of smallpox—sent some 10 percent of the empire's subjects to their graves, while an unknown pathogen, responsible for the Plague of Cyprian (249–62), had a similar impact. The Plague of Justinian (541–9) marked an early appearance of the hyper-deadly bacterium *Yersinia pestis*, which returned to cause the Black Death of the 1340s. The effect of these huge population losses on the overall economy was devastating.

A further cause—and symptom—of Roman decline was raiding and settlement by warrior groups from the east, which the empire also struggled to prevent. The *limes* had always been more of a sieve than a shield: cross-border trading thrived, with Romans offering the "barbarians" (the Latin term for foreigners) arms, precious metals, luxury goods, and wine in return for slaves, animals, and woodland products. From the late second century, this peaceful exchange turned into something more violent and disruptive. German attacks on the wealthy Roman cities behind the *limes* grew more frequent, forcing city-dwellers to build their own fortifications.

Enter the Franks

"I am a Frank, a Roman citizen, and a soldier in arms"
Inscription found in the Roman city of Aquincum
(modern-day Budapest)

The Franks were the most significant of these raiders. Their origins are obscure. Later medieval chroniclers claimed they were a band of refugees from the legendary city of Troy, but the truth seems rather more mundane. They first appeared in the second century as a loose coalition of German warbands regularly looting Gaulish cities and carrying their booty back across the border. By the late third century, they had settled on the near side of the Rhine. Rome made the best of a bad situation, granting the settlers land rights and political autonomy in return for military assistance against other foes. Soon, Rome was recruiting these barbarians into the empire's own army.

The wealth of Gaul's cities continued to attract raiders from the east long after the initial attacks. But factors far beyond the empire were driving migrants to its borders. A more unsettled climate seems to have disrupted the ecology of the vast steppe grasslands that stretch across Eurasia from Hungary to Manchuria. Nomadic tribes moved westward, displacing others and piling up population levels behind the *limes.*

Coming to Armorica

While most raiders and settlers came to Gaul from eastern Europe, a smaller current of migrants trickled in from the British Isles to the north. From the late fourth century, Celtic refugees from Cornwall, Ireland, Wales, and Scotland fled the raids of the Germanic Angles and Saxons, following old maritime trading routes south to the Armorican peninsula. This far-western tip of France was only lightly Romanized. By the sixth century its provincial name of Armorica was edged out by Britannia—or *Bretagne*, as it became. Celtic missionaries would play a major role in Christianizing the peninsula. Breton cities named after Welsh saints include Saint-Malo, Saint-Brieuc, and Saint-Pol-de-Léon. The "Brythonic" Welsh and Cornish languages also merged with pre-Roman Celtic to create the Breton language, still spoken in the region.

As more and more women and children joined these migrating warbands, they began to look less like bloodthirsty raiders and more like hapless refugees seeking new homes. In 406, a huge population surge overwhelmed the defensive cordon on the Rhine. Tribal groups from the middle Danube region joined Visigoth warbands already plundering the Italian peninsula. Rome was sacked in 410. Other Visigoth groups moved southwest, some settling to form the kingdom of Aquitaine, others pressing on to join the Alani and Suebi in the Iberian peninsula. The Vandals even reached Africa.

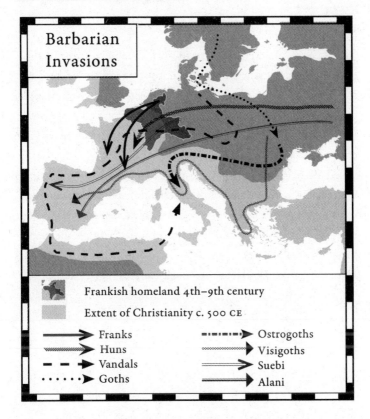

The Huns, the most imposing of these nomadic groupings, broke through from the eastern steppes. But their incursion was short-lived. In 451, at the battle of the Catalaunian Fields near Châlons-en-Champagne, the Roman general Aetius defeated their leader Attila, forcing them to retreat. Despite representing the last vestiges of Roman authority, Aetius's victorious army included a wide assortment of barbarian contingents, especially

Visigoths. In this restless swirl of peoples on the move, the old distinction between Romans and barbarians was eroding fast.

Picking Over the Spoils

Roman emperors were by now wholly incapable of arresting these migratory surges. Their power in Europe had been weakened by the creation in 330 of a new imperial center in Constantinople, modern-day Istanbul. This eastern "Byzantine" empire continued to thrive, but in the west the end was nigh. In 476, the last emperor in Rome was overthrown.

At its height, the Roman empire's vast networks opened up avenues for foreign trade, military adventure, and distant cultural encounters on a scale the Gauls and their descendants would not experience for another millennium or more. Now, as the empire broke in two and then lost its western half, their horizons narrowed. In effect, Gaul had been deglobalized.

The power vacuum left by Rome did, however, present a golden opportunity for the Franks. Already well established within the *limes*, they chose to stay put while other barbarian tribes were on the move. Over the course of the fifth century, one Frankish sub-group, the Salians, gradually imposed their authority on their neighbors. In 486, their leader Clovis defeated the pretender to the imperial crown, the Roman general Syagrius, in the battle of Soissons. It was a case of a Romanized barbarian prevailing over a barbarized Roman.

Clovis went on to conquer the Alamanni, the Burgundians, and the Visigoths to the south, choosing Paris as the capital of a by-now extensive Frankish kingdom. By the mid-sixth century, his dynasty would rule an area that covered a large proportion of the old western Roman empire.

Rule of the Long-Haired Kings

The signet ring of Clovis's father, Childeric, showing the flowing locks characteristic of the Merovingian dynasty

Clovis was the first of the so-called Merovingians, who derived their name from Merowech, a fantastical half-human, half-divine ancestor. More importantly, he styled himself "king of the Francs" (*rex Francorum*). The Latin term would be employed by French rulers well into the Middle Ages and was retained on royal coinage until the eighteenth century.

The Merovingians, later dubbed "the long-haired kings" on account of their distinctive hairstyle, took their recently conquered territories in a new political direction, swiveling away from the Mediterranean and the south toward the east. But the scale and nature of these changes were not immediately apparent, as the Merovingians continued to stress their Roman heritage and credentials. The Frankish civil law code issued around 500—the Salian or Salic Law—was written in Latin. Clovis's conversion in 508 to Christianity, Rome's state religion, was another marker of continuity. This was particularly important south of the Loire, for it ensured that rulers retained the support of bishops, who had become the most powerful members of the elite in former *civitates*.

Despite the regime's early emphasis on its *Romanitas*, it grew progressively more Germanic in character as time wore on. Archaeology and place-names suggest the Frankish presence was strongest in a dense strip of German-speaking territory between 60 and 150 miles west of the Rhine. New patterns of landownership here effaced the pre-existing villa system and shifted more land into Frankish hands. Away from these heartlands, however,

Merovingian authority waned. On the map, the dimensions of the Frankish kingdom look impressive, but size did not equate to real power. As time went on, the regime became ever more fragile.

Kingdom of the Franks
Under the Merovingians

Crumbling Foundations

The seeds of Merovingian weakness germinated while Clovis was still warm in his grave. At his death, the territories he had amassed were divided among his four sons. This practice of partible inheritance was to remain an Achilles heel of the dynasty and its successors, causing repeated fracturings of the Frankish *imperium* over the next centuries. The kingdom's main territorial blocs of Austrasia to the east, Neustria to the west, and Burgundy and

Aquitaine south of the Loire provoked continuous intra-familial strife, with numerous competing heirs at each other's throats.

Fragmentation of authority was evident from the top to the bottom of the Merovingian system. The Pax Romana had brought a significant peace dividend and its demise hit the economy hard. With many rural areas in a state of chronic insecurity, trade collapsed, agriculture stagnated, population levels declined, and cities fell into serious disrepair. The state's tax base shrank so sharply that rulers resorted to paying their war-band followers with shares in plundered goods or gifts of territory.

This new gift economy further deepened the fractures caused by dynastic squabbling. Powerful alliances of local notables resisted any strengthening of royal power. From the early seventh century, kingly authority began to be usurped by the stewards of their royal estates, the so-called Mayors of the Palace. These men became effective viceroys, performing executive and military functions, while the kings were confined to ceremonial roles. The early eighth century saw a succession of so-called *rois fainéants*—"do-nothing kings"—chronically unable to impose their political will.

> There was nothing left for the king to do but to be content with his name of king, his flowing hair, and long beard, to sit on his throne and play the ruler. . . . He had nothing that he could call his own beyond this vain title of King and the precarious support allowed by the Mayor of the Palace in his discretion, except a single country seat, that brought him but a very small income.
>
> Einhard (ninth century) on the last of
> the Merovingian *rois fainéants*

Though it touched on some truths, Einhard's withering description is certainly overdrawn. It was a propaganda piece in praise of Charles the Great, best known as Charlemagne, the most illustrious of the Merovingians' successors.

The Rise of the Carolingians

The Arnulfing dynasty that later became known as the Carolingians had been steadily growing stronger at Merovingian expense. As Mayor of the Palace in Austrasia, Charles Martel (Charlemagne's

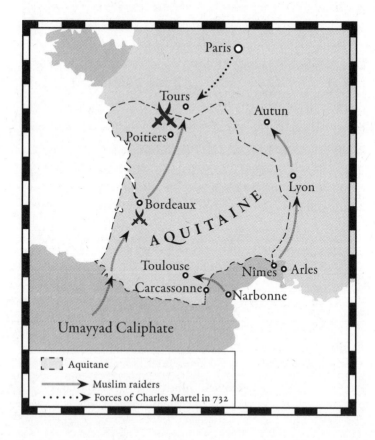

grandfather) extended his political and military influence across Frankish lands and east into Germany, forcing his new subjects to adopt Christianity. To the south, he also faced up to the rising military threat of Islam.

The period following the death of the Prophet Muhammad in 632 in Medina had seen the extraordinary rise of Islam as a global superpower. From its heartland in the east, the Umayyad caliphate swept across Mediterranean Africa, moving north in 711 to overthrow the Visigothic kingdom on the Iberian peninsula and establish the Islamic state of Al-Andalus. In 719, Umayyad forces occupied the former Roman city of Narbonne, using it as a base from which to launch raids into the French interior.

In 732, Charles Martel defeated an Umayyad army at the battle of Tours (also known as the battle of Poitiers). The battlefield was the furthest north the Arab forces would get. Charles Martel's victory over the Moors, as they were more generally known in Spain, was seen for centuries as an iconic turning point: the moment medieval Christendom was "saved" from militant Islam. Yet the Muslim incursions into France could be considered less an attempt to extend Islamic rule north than another example of the opportunistic plunder-raiding endemic to the region. Indeed, the Umayyad caliphs were unlikely to have viewed Frankish Europe as especially worth conquering: the warmer, wealthier south was a much more attractive target. Culturally, too, the Arab world had more than an edge over these northern backwaters. The Roman intellectual inheritance was far stronger in Islamic culture than in western Europe. In discussing the Franks, Islamic writers stooped to condescend.

> Their bodies have become enormous, their humor dry, their morals crude, their intellect stupid and their tongues sluggish. Their color has become excessively white.... Those of them who are furthest to the north are the most subject to stupidity, grossness and brutishness.
>
> al-Masudi (tenth-century), on the Franks

Seen in this light, victory at Tours in 732 had a downside for the Franks. For several centuries, the Christian west would only rarely glimpse an intellectual and cultural world that far outshone it. Moreover, Christianity was vastly the more intolerant of the two faiths at this time. The rulers of Al-Andalus permitted Christians to live according to their own rites, while religious toleration was anathema to Frankish rulers. The Carolingians forced pagan Germans to convert on pain of death.

Carolingian Consolidation

Extent of Western Roman Empire
Extent of Carolingian Empire

Tours was the making of *Carolus Martellus* ("Charles the Hammer") and the dynasty that took his name. As their territory grew, the Carolingians consolidated Christianity not only in the northeast (Frisia, Saxony) and the southeast (Bavaria, Carinthia), but also in Italy and the Spanish March. At its peak, the empire covered around two thirds of the former western Roman empire north of the Mediterranean.

The Carolingians' vigorous promotion of the Roman faith earned the gratitude of the papacy in Rome. In 751, Pope Zachary acknowledged the debt by giving his blessing to Martel's son Pepin (Charlemagne's father) when he deposed the last Merovingian ruler, Childeric III, and despatched him to a monastery. The pope anointed Pepin sole king of the Franks, identifying him as God's chosen ruler. In 754, Pepin handsomely returned the favor when Rome found itself threatened by the Lombards, a Germanic group who had installed themselves throughout the Italian peninsula. Pope Stephen II ventured north of the Alps to plead for Frankish military help. Pepin obliged, and went on to defeat the Lombards in battle.

Papal endorsement of the Carolingians reached its zenith in a striking coup de théâtre in Rome on Christmas Day 800, when Pope Leo III crowned Pepin's son and heir Charlemagne *imperator,* or Roman emperor. Charles the Great would seek throughout his reign to mark continuity with the last, Christian phase of the Roman empire.

"Charles Was Large and Strong"

Erected in 1882, the bronze statue of Charlemagne that stands outside Notre-Dame cathedral in Paris is, like that of Vercingetorix, a work of vivid imagination. Though no contemporary portrait exists, his chronicler Einhard's description—to which tradition has added a magnificent beard—is certainly colorful.

"Charles was large and strong, and of lofty stature, though not disproportionately tall (his height is well known to have been seven times the length of his foot); the upper part of his head was round, his eyes very large and animated, nose a little long, hair fair, and face laughing and merry. Thus his appearance was always stately and dignified, whether he was standing or sitting; although his neck was thick and somewhat short, and his belly rather prominent; but the symmetry of the rest of his body concealed these defects. His gait was firm, his whole carriage manly, and his voice clear, but not so strong as his size led one to expect."

The statue was one of relatively few in Paris to survive destruction by the Nazis in the 1940s, highlighting the Frankish emperor's place in German as well as French culture. Hitler's "Third" Reich saw Charlemagne's empire as the First.

A Clerical Renaissance

Charlemagne viewed antiquity through the prism of the Church, putting the Christian faith as well as the Latin language at the heart of most of his reforms. He boosted the activity of monastic libraries, almost the only places in western Europe where the classical heritage survived, ensuring that copyists targeted works by church fathers as well as manuscripts by classical authors. At his favored residence at Aix-la-Chapelle (today's Aachen in Germany) he founded a school of learning, summoning the finest scholars of the age to work under his chief adviser, the Anglo-Saxon monk Alcuin of York.

Monasteries, chapels, and cathedrals were Charlemagne's architectural predilection. As shown here in his palace chapel at Aix-la-Chapelle, his reign marked the development of a new "Romanesque" style.

The Carolingian elite was schooled in Latin, which became the language of government throughout the empire. A standardized version was enforced, closer to the language of the ancients than to "popular" or "vulgar" Latin (though Charlemagne was pragmatic enough to instruct clerics that they should use "rustic Roman" forms in their sermons). The emperor also presided over a revival of interest in classical art that infused the illuminated manuscripts, frescoes, mosaics, and religious architecture of the era.

Things Fall Apart

The imperial unity achieved under Charlemagne did not last long. Despite his admiration for all things Roman, the emperor clung to the ingrained Frankish custom of partible inheritance, insisting that his domains be divided among his legitimate sons after his death, which came in 814. Problems were initially averted by the demise of two of his three heirs, but in 817 the remaining son, Louis the Pious, determined that when he died he too would divide the empire among his own legitimate issue.

As after Clovis's death, generations of dynastic squabbling ensued. When Louis died in 840, his three sons fought like cats in a sack over the sharing of their birthright. Eventually they hit upon a tripartite division, organized as long north–south strips, as set out in the 843 Treaty of Verdun. A middle kingdom was created, stretching from the Low Countries down to Rome and the Spanish March. Its northern part became known as Lotharingia, after its first ruler Lothair. He also assumed the title of emperor, though this conferred little real lordship over the territories assigned to his brothers. Louis the German took East Francia, which stretched from Saxony to Bavaria, while Charles the Bald received West Francia.

Swearing in Proto-French: The Strasbourg Oaths (842)

Eighteen months before Verdun, Charles of West Francia and Louis of East Francia met at Strasbourg to sign a military pact. Each swore their loyalty oath in a language the other's followers could understand: Louis in an evolving form of Old French, and Charles in a German dialect. The Romance and Germanic passages in the Oaths prefigure a cultural divergence between the two sides of the empire—or France and Germany, as they would become.

Even so, the linguistic map of West Francia was still very much in flux. Latin remained the language of government, law and religious life. While "popular Latin" was mutating into versions of Old French, other languages in the south, such as Occitan, Franco-Provençal, and Catalan, were developing alongside it. Breton was spoken in the far west and Basque deep in the southwest. The north contained speakers of evolving Germanic languages such as Frisian, Dutch, and Flemish. And as we shall see, Old Norse was about to arrive in Normandy too.

The Norsemen Cometh

If the linguistic map was fragmenting, so, too, was the political landscape, following a fresh wave of plundering raids across the empire in the late eighth century. There were three main groups of pagan raiders: the Magyars, the Saracens, and the Vikings. East Francia and Lotharingia bore the brunt of attacks by the Magyars, warlike nomads originally from the Urals. West Francia was more affected by the Saracens, as Muslims were increasingly called. Incursions from Al-Andalus were now bolstered by seaborne attacks on Frankish cities along the Mediterranean coast. A Saracen force established an operational base on high ground near Saint-Tropez, from which they were only finally evicted in 972.

But by far the most formidable of the invaders were the Vikings, sea-raiders from Scandinavia who rapidly established themselves as a global power. Their raids reached deep into Frankish territory and far beyond: to Iceland and Greenland in the west, to the Iberian peninsula and the Mediterranean in the south, and along Russian river valleys as far as the Black Sea. They were the first Europeans since the Romans to make their presence felt on the three continents of Europe, Asia, and Africa. Indeed, they may well have reached a fourth: the Viking explorer Leif Erikson is thought to have set up a colony at "Vinland" in present-day Newfoundland.

The Vikings had begun raiding up and down the west coast of France in the 790s. As the ninth century wore on, their longboats penetrated far inland along navigable rivers such as the Loire and the Seine, terrorizing cities and the wealthy yet vulnerable monasteries outside their walls. They besieged Paris and its environs repeatedly from the 840s onward, sacking the powerful *extramuros* ("outside the walls") monastery of Saint-Germain-des-Prés.

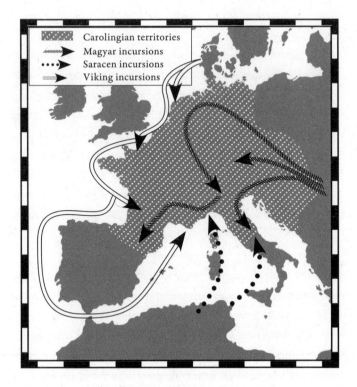

Despite their initial fondness for hit-and-run tactics, the Vikings soon began to settle—most notably in Normandy, where the duchy owes it origins to raiders bribed by Frankish rulers to cease their attacks. In 867, Charles the Bald handed territory around Cherbourg to a Viking group on condition they converted to Christianity and helped fight off other warbands. In 911, Charles the Simple granted the Viking chieftain Rollo rights of settlement in the lower Seine valley on similar terms, demanding conversion and an oath of loyalty to the king of the Franks. By 933, more or less all of modern-day Normandy was in the hands of the Vikings—or *Normands* (Normans), as the Franks called these Norsemen.

Fragments of a Future France

Failure to repel these multiple invasions caused a widespread loss of faith in the empire and its rulers. In 888, West Francian nobles took matters into their own hands, even electing a king—Odo (or Eudes), count of Paris—from their own ranks. For the best part of a century afterward, the West Francian crown would be batted like a shuttlecock between the Carolingians and the Robertians, the family of Odo. The kingdom began to fragment into sizeable territories—notably Aquitaine, Burgundy, Brittany, Champagne, Flanders, and Provence—ruled by a duke or even king. Below the ducal level, smaller, often autonomous areas such as *comtés* (areas ruled by a *comte,* or count) emerged in many places.

The shaky state of the imperial economy only encouraged this political fragmentation. Curiously, for a brief period in the tenth century, Viking plundering contributed to a surge in prosperity as it freed gold and silver from churches, monasteries, and noble estates and released them into wider circulation. A lively trade in enslaved Slavs, Magyars, and other conquered peoples at the imperial frontier also brought in revenue from the Byzantine empire. Yet the underlying weakness of the economy soon made itself felt. Territorial expansion ground to a halt, as Charlemagne's heirs spent more time fighting each other than seeking to expand or defend their empire.

Lotharingia and the Middle Kingdom

Born at Verdun in 842, the kingdom of "Middle Francia" briefly spanned a huge strip of Europe from the North Sea to the Mediterranean before falling afoul of the dynastic tradition of partible inheritance. After 855, Lothair II retained only the northern part, known as Lotharingia,

West Francia, the Middle Kingdom, and East Francia after 843, as the rough outlines of a future France and Germany were becoming visible: The empire that Otto would proclaim in the east in 962 became known as the "Holy Roman Empire" from the thirteenth century.

which was subsequently nibbled away at by France, the Holy Roman Empire, Burgundy in the south, and the Netherlands to the northwest. Yet remnants of Lotharingia managed to survive for nearly a millennium as the duchy of Lorraine (Lothringen in German) by playing off these more powerful neighbors against one other. Lorraine was one of the last pieces of the hexagonal jigsaw to fall into place when it was formally incorporated into France in 1766, finally withdrawing from the Holy Roman Empire. Even then, its story was not quite over. Lorraine passed into the hands of Germany in 1870–18711 before returning to France in 1918–1919. This mixed cultural heritage persists to this day, with German spoken as the main local language in the northern and western parts of the region.

Weakness at the imperial center was, moreover, highlighted in 962 by the unilateral decision by Otto, king of the East Franks, to assume the title of emperor. With a few exceptions such as Lorraine, the German monarch had little interest in the territories of West Francia. As the millennium ended, it was by no means clear that a common future awaited this mess of disparate territories. The Carolingian framework of empire had gone. Even though on paper the rough contours of the future Hexagon were becoming visible, in practice whole regions looked for authority to leaders other than a king. Often this was no more than a local lord. In addition, much of Flanders and the northeast, as well as southern territories on the left bank of the Rhône, seemed to belong less to West Francia than to the Germanic empire, while the Languedoc region was within the gravitational pull of the Iberian peninsula. There was little sign that the West Francian polity was strong enough to resist these distant forces of attraction. France was still to be made.

CHAPTER 2

THE LUCK OF THE CAPETIANS

France Emergent (1000–1500)

In 1000, France was little more than a shaky outline on a map. By 1500, it was a unified political and economic powerhouse, with a strong cultural, artistic, intellectual, and linguistic profile. This transformation was a stop-start process, full of diversions, backslidings, and challenges. The shape and substance of the kingdom fluctuated wildly over the centuries and was perennially unpacked and stitched together again in ways that defy easy summary. All major land frontiers shifted over the period, while very few regions stayed firmly under royal authority throughout. Even Paris, France's capital, spent fifteen years under the rule of the king of England.

Despite the extraordinary turbulence of the times, which on occasion brought France close to extinction, by 1500 the kingdom had developed a preening presence in Europe and was developing a role on the world stage, particularly in and around the Mediterranean. If France had been on the receiving end of history in the previous millennium, by 1500 it was setting the terms for its own development.

Hugh: The First Capetian

It was around this time that France acquired its name. Initially the poor cousin of the imperial territories of East Francia and Lotharingia, by the late tenth century West Francia had the term *Francia* to itself, Otto's eastern holdings generally being referred to as "the Empire."

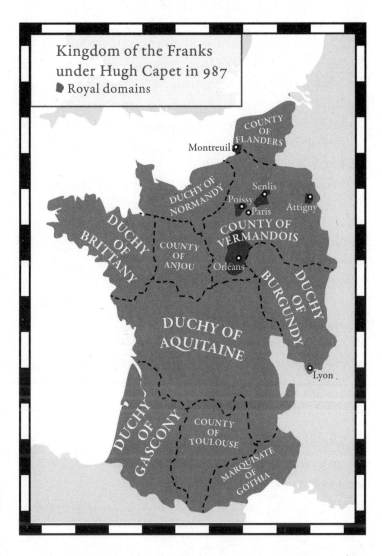

Kingdom of the Franks under Hugh Capet in 987

🔖 Royal domains

COUNTY OF FLANDERS

Montreuil

DUCHY OF NORMANDY

Senlis

Poissy

Paris

Attigny

COUNTY OF VERMANDOIS

DUCHY OF BRITTANY

COUNTY OF ANJOU

Orléans

DUCHY OF BURGUNDY

DUCHY OF AQUITAINE

Lyon

DUCHY OF GASCONY

COUNTY OF TOULOUSE

MARQUISATE OF GOTHIA

In 987, an assembly of nobles met at Noyon in Picardy (the frontier area north of Paris) to elect the first king of the Franks (*rex Francorum*), elevating the Robertian magnate Hugh Capet from the status of duke (*dux Francorum*). Later chroniclers have debated whether this year should perhaps mark the birth of the French nation. Yet Hugh's lands comprised not West Francia as a whole but merely some scattered holdings in what became the Ile de France, centered on Paris, the Frankish capital since Clovis. To contemporaries, Noyon appeared less like the launch of a fresh dynasty than another chapter in the sad story of Frankish decline in the west.

Indeed, it was Hugh's weakness, not his strength, that secured him the crown. With his diminutive territorial base, he posed less of an obvious threat to the magnates who elected him than his Carolingian rivals, who came with heavy dynastic baggage. The nobles would also accept Hugh's teenage son Robert as successor without debate in 996, quietly abandoning the practice of electing a ruler and paving the way to inherited kingship—along with the principle of primogeniture.

From this unassuming start, the Capetians would go on to produce an unbroken and largely unchallenged line of direct heirs for more than three hundred years. With later shifts to the collateral Valois and Bourbon lines, the dynasty would effectively last eight centuries and produce more than forty monarchs. This extraordinary stroke of luck meant that the French monarchy effectively waved goodbye to Frankish partible inheritance and all the divisive problems that went with it.

France's royal dynasties since Clovis

Merovingians	496–751
Carolingians	751–987
Capetians	987–1328
Valois	1328–1589
Bourbons	1589–1792 and 1815–30

At this time the peculiar, cellular structure of feudalism was spreading across Europe. A military elite of noble vassals occupied the top layer of this pyramidal hive of feudal service and obligation. These magnates were formally the king's vassals and owed him the feudal oath of fealty—or allegiance—by which they swore to defend and support him, if necessary by *main-forte* or strength of arms. Beneath them in the feudal pyramid were their own vassals, who might serve their lords as knights but who also owned lands and prized their independence. At the base of the pyramid,

as ever, were the peasants who tilled the soil as serfs.

The symbolic authority of the Capetian rulers was unchallengeable. Converting it into real power was a different matter. In reality, a handful of West Francian nobles possessed far more extensive territories than their Capetian monarch, in many cases received as gifts of land from past Merovingian and Carolingian rulers. Often these domains were hereditary, too, giving their owners the independence necessary to build rival polities to the crown, with their own tax and justice systems and private armies. Capetian efforts to master these unruly noble elements was complicated by the fact that the magnates themselves had to deal with trouble below.

Due to his meager territorial possessions, the king had to rely on a honeycomb of personal relationships, rivalries, and other intermediaries to influence the wider population of his kingdom. He also had to cope with powerful neighbors. On France's eastern flank, the Emperor enjoyed authority throughout Lotharingia, which was composed of myriad fragmented territories from Flanders to Provence. In the far west there was the independent-minded duchy of Brittany. And on the Mediterranean coastline the king had to compete with the counts of Barcelona and then the kings of Aragon, who aimed to increase their power in Languedoc and Provence.

Between Angevins and Empire

Yet the most egregious threat to Capetian power came from within France itself, in the shape of the duchy of once-Viking Normandy. The conquest of England in 1066 by Duke William produced an

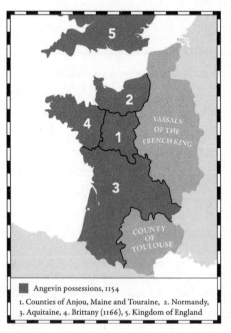

Angevin possessions, 1154
1. Counties of Anjou, Maine and Touraine, 2. Normandy,
3. Aquitaine, 4. Brittany (1166), 5. Kingdom of England

anomalous situation whereby a vassal of the Capetian king ruled one of France's biggest rivals. The Normans extended their possessions on the European mainland too. In 1154, the Angevin ("from Anjou") Henry II of England acceded not only to the English crown but also to a huge expanse of land on France's western seaboard, which ran from Normandy down to Aquitaine and Gascony in the south and across to the Auvergne in the Massif Central. France risked being squashed between two juggernauts, the English to the north and west and the German empire to the east.

As it turned out, France's struggle against this emerging Anglo-Norman state was the making of the Capetians. Over the period from 1159 to 1299, they gradually pushed the English back. At the battle of Bouvines in 1214, Philip II—or Philip Augustus, as he came to be called—inflicted an epic defeat on the English and their Flemish and German allies, after which the English crown had to renounce most of its continental territories, retaining only Guyenne in the southwest.

The struggle with England would flare up again in the fourteenth century. But the spectacular victory at Bouvines gave the Capetians considerable prestige and helped consolidate their power across France. At the turn of the millennium, the new dynasty had seemed very much down on its luck. Within the space of a few generations, Hugh Capet's descendants displayed a striking ability to surf the waves of political fortune, and in a way that registered on the map.

Weaponized Christianity

The new millennium seemed to herald a new sense of security across northern Europe, as the waves of plunder and invasion that had blighted earlier centuries finally subsided. The Magyars settled down and the Vikings stopped pillaging. Even more importantly, a turning of the tide saw the Christian powers begin to repel the forces of Islam.

The ejection of Saracen pirates from Provence in 972 marked the beginning of a general European assault on the Muslim

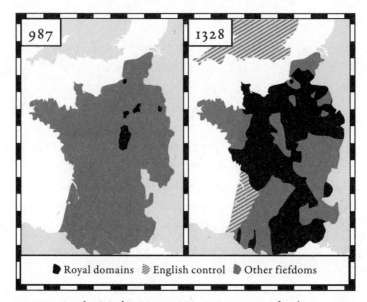

● Royal domains ◪ English control ◗ Other fiefdoms

presence in the Mediterranean. In a succession of military operations that would last centuries, the Spanish *Reconquista* began to expel the Moors from the Iberian peninsula. Norman Vikings, who had occupied southern Italy, switched their attention to the conquest of Arab Sicily. Meanwhile, the French became leading participants in the anti-Islamic Crusades.

Launched in 1095 by Pope Urban II, a native of Châtillon in Champagne, the Crusades had as their initial aim the recapture of the Holy Land and protection of the region's Christians from the advancing Seljuk Turks. They would redefine European civilization in the two centuries of religious conflict that followed. The Greeks and Romans had regarded anyone who did not speak their language or share their wider values as a "barbarian." By the eleventh century, a new and enduring polarity had emerged, namely between Christians on the one hand and "infidels" or "heretics" on the other.

Much of the impetus for the Crusades came from the papacy. From the late tenth century, successive popes had been promoting the "Truce of God" movement, which sought to recreate the Pax Romana in Europe by making the conduct of warfare less barbaric. This grew into a wider strategy to redirect violence outward, against Muslims and others deemed spiritually unworthy.

The French imprinted themselves powerfully on this crusading movement. The church council that launched the first crusade was held in the French city of Clermont. French monarchs participated wholeheartedly throughout, King Louis IX (St Louis) leading the last two crusades in person. Perhaps half of the French nobility went crusading at some point, or else fought the Moors on the Iberian peninsula. After the capture of Jerusalem in 1099, it was largely French nobles who organized the four "crusader states" of

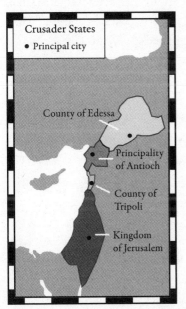

Jerusalem, Antioch, Edessa, and Tripoli. They became known collectively as *France d'outre-mer* ("Overseas France"), with French their common language—or Occitan, in the case of Tripoli. The upper echelons of the crusading orders of Knights Hospitaller created to protect pilgrims and local Christians were also of mainly Frankish provenance. Revealingly, the generic term that Muslims used for crusaders was the Persian word *farang* ("Frank").

Crusader States
● Principal city

County of Edessa

Principality of Antioch

County of Tripoli

Kingdom of Jerusalem

The three orders or estates: *oratores* ("those who pray"); *bellatores* ("those who fight," comprising the noble military elite); and the third estate, *laboratores* ("those who work," or pretty much everyone else).

The alliance between France and the papacy during the Crusades was nothing new. Frankish kings had been hand-in-glove with the church since the days of Clovis. They accepted the church's primary position in society, based on the classic description of the three orders, with the nobility and commoners as the second and third estates.

The church suffused all aspects of French society. Besides holding extensive lands and property rights, it also took a tithe (that is, a tenth) of agricultural produce. Burgundy had become a beacon of western monasticism: the Cluniac order, founded at Cluny in 909, and the Cistercians, established in Cîteaux in 1098, were the most influential monastic networks in Europe. After an electoral squabble over the papal title, the French crown would even shelter a rival pope at Avignon for much of the fourteenth century. Kings began adding to their titles the sobriquet *Rex Christianissimus* ("Most Christian King"), which the papacy endorsed.

A Legacy of Violence

Whether for France, Europe, or Christendom, the military campaigns were hardly an unqualified success. If anything, the reverse is true. By 1291, all of *France d'outre-mer* was in the hands of the Mamluk Sultanate. The violence at times was horrific. Muslims were the prime casualties, but civilians of all religions suffered. During the infamous Fourth Crusade, crusading forces sacked the Christian city of Constantinople in 1204, inflicting damage from which the Byzantine empire never fully recovered.

Despite their ultimate failure and cost in human lives, the Crusades hugely boosted the prestige of the Capetians. Successive rulers were represented as paragons of Christian virtue. Even before the long reign of Saint Louis (1226–1270), the dynasty's propagandists were highlighting the special favor the Capetians derived from God. Abbé Suger of Saint-Denis claimed that the coronation ritual originating with Clovis gave French monarchs divine, miraculous healing powers over the "King's Evil" (the tubercular illness, scrofula). The ceremonial practice of the "Royal Touch" for scrofular victims would survive into the nineteenth century.

A Bouquet of Louis

French history boasts seventeen kings named Louis as well as one royal pretender, "Louis XVII," the uncrowned son of the guillotined Louis XVI, who died as a child in prison. No other name found such royal favor, though Charles is a close contender with ten. In the early days of monarchy, "Louis" invited associations with Clovis, itself a Gallcized version of Hlodovig (which became Ludwig in German). Later kings probably looked more to the saintly Louis IX following his canonization in the thirteenth century, though the renown of Louis XIV, the Sun King, gave the ancient name a late boost in popularity. From early on, the Capetians associated their kinship with the emblem of a lily, the fleur-de-lys. So if one were to invent a collective noun for Louis, it might be a bouquet.

Enemies Within

The Capetians did not confine their crusading to foreign shores. The *bellatores* ("fighters") also campaigned against religious minorities closer to home. In southwest France, the so-called Albigensian Crusade was launched in 1209 against the Cathars and the wealthy magnates who protected them. The counts of Toulouse had tolerated the spread of Catharism, a dualistic belief in a warring spirit realm and material world. They were already

The fortress-like appearance of Albi cathedral is no accident. Built in the late thirteenth century in the heartland of the Albigensian heresy, it sent out a powerful repressive message to anyone tempted to stray back toward Cathar beliefs.

notorious for protecting local Jewish communities, who in turn were also accused of aiding and abetting the Cathar heresy.

Although it was Pope Innocent III who announced the crusade, it was French kings and their minions who directed operations against the Cathars, who referred to themselves as Good Christians. For two decades, military campaigns targeted the wealthy cities of Toulouse, Carcassonne, and Béziers, leading to civilian massacres and huge property confiscations—materially enriching noblemen from northern France, as well as their sovereign.

Militant Christianity allowed the Capetian dynasty to escape from its West Francian box, helping it not only to consolidate power within France but also to exert its influence across Europe and beyond. By the early fourteenth century, an Italian chronicler could remark that, "In all of Christendom the king of France has no equal."

Jews in Medieval France

Jewish trading communities had existed in Gaul since Roman times, rubbing shoulders with Christian populations for the best part of a millennium. The new crusading ethos changed that. The massacres of Jews in the Rhineland by zealous troops in 1096 on their way east for the First Crusade were a sign of things to come. Traditional complaints about Jews as usurers were joined by darker mutterings about the alleged ritual murder of Christian children. Jews were obliged in many cities to wear a yellow badge as a mark of their outsider status. Although Jewish money-lending was important enough to make cash-strapped monarchs hesitate, in 1306 the crown took the plunge and expelled Jews outright from the whole of France, seizing their property. A more definitive expulsion was decreed in 1394. It would be centuries before large numbers of Jews returned to France.

An Age of Smiles

The famous smiling angel sculpture placed on the cathedral at Reims around 1240 has been hailed as marking the invention of the smile in western art. Its sweet and unclouded facial gesture also stands as a worthy symbol of a more optimistic world view that was emerging at this time. And times were smiling with special kindness on France.

A dramatic improvement in climate helped to invigorate the economy. Beginning in the tenth century and peaking in the thirteenth, the Medieval Warm Period seemed particularly favorable to Europe, giving France and its neighbors a competitive advantage over the rest of the globe. Longer growing seasons meant more food, while milder conditions allowed peripheral lands and forests to be cultivated. Marshland was drained and sea and river ports were built across the country.

A warmer climate also provided a demographic stimulus. France's population tripled in the first three centuries of the millennium, from about five or six million in 1000 to fifteen million or more by 1300. Agricultural production kept pace, better harvests enabling the extra mouths to be fed. Improved agrarian technology played a part too. Use of the iron plough, suitable for heavy northern soils, was widespread even before the onset of warming, but it was now joined by more efficient wind and water mills and refined crop rotation systems.

The Lure of the Mediterranean

The traditional focus of Frankish power had always been central and eastern Europe, but as Capetian authority grew it shifted southward toward the Mediterranean. Here, the French were able to piggyback on the dynamism of the Italian city-states of Venice, Pisa, and Genoa, which formed the leading edge of European commerce and finance. From the twelfth century, the fairs of Champagne (the region, not the wine) brought the people and wares of northern and southern Europe together. Italians traded their own manufactured products as well as commodities sourced from across the Mediterranean and beyond, from medicinal drugs to exotic silks and spices. In return, they took back surplus wheat, Flemish woolen goods and more. They helped turn Constantinople and Alexandria into busy entrepôts, fed by the dense web of land and maritime trade routes from the Far East known collectively as the Silk Road.

Road to Riches

Originating in Roman times, the fortunes of the Silk Road had waxed and waned through the first millennium. In the thirteenth century, the sprawling Mongol Empire brought a measure of security to these trans-Eurasian trade routes that enabled them to thrive. Not only was silk carried westward but also metalware, precious stones, and dyes. Moreover, a "spice route" from Indonesia and India supplied sugar and incense, as well as pepper, cinnamon, nutmeg, cassia, and other ingredients.

It was while on crusade that many French nobles discovered these exotic commodities. They brought their newly acquired tastes back home. In order to afford luxury goods, landlords squeezed their estates for income, often allowing peasants to pay cash rents in place of feudal labor obligations. Nobles also nurtured markets in towns and villages near their castles. To cater to elite demand, gardeners experimented with medicinal herbs and other plants from the Levant and from Islamic Sicily and Spain—spinach, apricots, peaches, pistachios, mulberries—that would become commonplace in time. At first, this rarefied traffic had little direct impact on the 90 percent or more of French people who scratched a living from the land. Over time, however, the trade in luxury goods permeated and stimulated the wider economy.

Cities and towns grew at a pace unparalleled since Roman times. Their character changed, too, from military, administrative, or religious hubs to commercial and manufacturing powerhouses. Many sought to establish themselves as communes with legal rights of self-government. They did this by acquiring a charter from a local lord, monastic foundation, regional magnate, or even the monarch himself. With their newfound autonomy, towns and cities began to act as players in their own right in regional and even national politics.

Europe's most important manufacturing region outside Italy was Flanders. Its fine cloth production, centered around Bruges, Ypres, and Ghent, reached across the frontier into Beauvais and Provins. Paris also acquired considerable renown as a center for the finishing work required for gold and silverware, jewelry, stained glass, illuminated (richly decorated) manuscripts, and fine paper. In the late twelfth century, it even began to manufacture silk, showing the role of the Silk Road in transporting know-how as well as material commodities. As in other towns and cities, a system of guilds developed to regulate these trades.

Medieval Guilds

Guilds were associations of merchants or artisans organized as legal corporations that managed members' professional interests and offered mutual aid and protection. Paris had well over three hundred guilds in the fourteenth century, while even average-sized towns might have had around a hundred. They ranged from workers in lowly trades—masons, weavers, and cobblers—to artisans producing luxury wares. Apart from their economic importance, guilds played an integral role in the public life of their home town: the coat of arms of the Parisian river merchants (pictured) became that of the city itself.

As towns and cities specialized, so, too, did regions. Normandy developed a strong dairy industry, the Ile de France grew grain, while wine production boomed in the Bordelais, Burgundy, and Alsace regions. While road conditions were improving, wine producers typically reached their markets through major river networks (from Alsace to northern France and Germany) or coastal shipping (from Bordeaux to England). Transporting hundreds of barrels of wine was cheaper and easier by water than overland, partly thanks to advances such as the compass, introduced to Europe by Arab navigators.

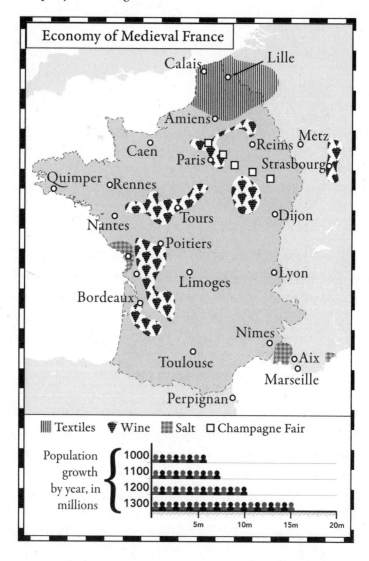

Economy of Medieval France

|||| Textiles   ▼ Wine   ▓ Salt   □ Champagne Fair

Population growth by year, in millions

1000

1100

1200

1300

5m   10m   15m   20m

Trading patterns slowly began to shift. Italian merchants opened a maritime route to northern Europe through the straits of Gibraltar, bypassing the Champagne fairs. Bruges emerged as the main hub for European trade, extending sea-routes into the north Atlantic and the Baltic. New port cities such as Seville, Lisbon and La Rochelle entered the trading loop. These new maritime routes gradually reshaped the commercial map of Europe.

Oc and Oil: The Emerging French Language

While Latin was still the language of church and state, French merchants would have spoken an array of Romance dialects, most notably Old French and Occitan. "Some say *oc*, others *oil*," the great Italian poet Dante wrote around 1305, expressing puzzlement at the different ways the French said "yes." He had put his finger on a major linguistic divide.

In the north, Old French had emerged from vulgar Latin, albeit with many geographically distinct variants—Francien around Paris, Picard in Picardy, Champenois, Lorrain, and so on. These northern territories of the *langue d'oil* were divided from the southern areas of the *langue d'oc* by a rough line running between La Rochelle and Turin. Here, the main language was Occitan. The divide extended well beyond France: Occitan was spoken in Spanish and Italian territories, while the *langue d'oil* could be heard in Lorraine, Burgundy, and parts of what is now Belgium under the authority of the Holy Roman Empire. It was a highly complex linguistic map and one that was evolving rapidly.

Ever since the Norman Conquest, depicted by the Bayeux Tapestry as pitching "Franci" against "Angli," the rulers of England had seen themselves as part of a francophone world. The Anglo-Norman dialect (a form of *langue d'oil*) remained the language of the elite for several centuries, evolving into "Insular" or Anglo-French. This became the language of government not only in England but also in the French southwest under the Plantagenets, while the Normans also carried the *langue d'oil* to southern Italy and Sicily as well as *France d'outre-mer*. Curiously, written French was used a century earlier in England than in France—it could even be regarded as the cradle of French literature, given the huge number of medieval mystery plays, lays, romances, saints' lives, and poetry that were produced in Anglo-French and read across the Channel.

Songs of Courtly Love and Slaughter

As the many, varied languages of France spilled over the boundaries of the French state, so, too, did its poetry and other literature. From the late eleventh century, Occitanian troubadour poems and songs emerged south of the Loire, spreading first through Spain and Italy and then into northern France and Germany. Troubadour poetry was closely associated with ducal and royal courts—an early practitioner was Richard, duke of Aquitaine, better known as King Richard "Lionheart" of England.

The vernacular poetry of the era celebrated a refined "courtly love" ethic that took the values of homage, loyalty, honor, and devotion inherent in the hyper-masculine feudal bond and focused them instead on a female love-object. Troubadour poems are steeped in the language of chivalry, as are the epics and *chansons de gestes* ("songs of heroic exploits") of the period. Characters act out idealized forms of chivalric behavior in a variety of settings, from the courts, caves, and mystical forests of the Arthurian romances to the mysterious backdrop of *France d'outre-mer*.

The Song of Roland, Islamophobic Knight

"The pagans are wrong and the Christians are right!" The battle cry of Charlemagne's paladin Roland in his famous

chanson de geste rings across the ages with its severely Manichean view of warfare and religion. Composed around 1100 and popular well into the sixteenth

Two soldiers leading two Muslim men before a king (c. 1290–1310)

century, "The Song of Roland" tells the story of the epic eighth-century battle at Roncevaux between Roland's heroic Franks and an invading Saracen army. The enemy are painted in the crudest colors—the Saracen warrior Abisme is "black as molten pitch," a man of evil character who "loves treason and murder better than all the gold of Galicia." Yet his worst trait, as the poet sees it, is

> paganism, for he "does not believe in God the son of the
> Virgin Mary." Though a triumph of the new literary art,
> the poetic defense of "sweet France" was built on the idea
> that the only good pagan was a dead one.

Debts to Antiquity—and Islam

Despite the overt Islamophobia of the "Song of Roland" and
other literary works, beneath the surface Europeans quietly bene-
fitted from the achievements of Islamic culture.

The learning of antiquity remained far more deeply rooted in
the Muslim world than in the Latin West. After the fall of the
Roman empire, Arabic had replaced Latin as the scientific *lingua
franca* across the Mediterranean, as Islamic regimes stockpiled and
translated vast troves of ancient Greek manuscripts. In places on
the Islamic frontier such as Toledo in Spain and Norman Sicily,
scholars began diligently copying and translating Plato, Aristotle,
Galen, and Hippocrates from Arabic into Latin. From the eleventh century, France and its European peers began to catch up on
what they had missed.

Universities led this mimetic mission. Many grew out of the
cathedral and monastic schools promoted during the Carolingian
renaissance, though the influence of the madrasas of Islamic Spain
cannot be dismissed. The university of Bologna, founded in 1088,
was Europe's first such formal institution, though some universi-
ty-style teaching was already taking place in Paris. In 1200, King
Philip Augustus gave royal backing to the city's teachers; in 1352,
a college was founded by Robert de Sorbon, whose name soon
became synonymous with the whole university, the Sorbonne.
Other French universities—at Toulouse, Orléans, Montpellier,
and Perpignan—soon followed.

Universities were divided into four faculties—theology (the most senior), law, medicine, and the arts—which were held to contain the sum total of permissible human knowledge. Their "universality" was also evident in their openness to all comers (anyone who knew Latin, that is, which excluded over 95 percent of the population). Many of the Sorbonne's greatest scholars were foreigners: Thomas Aquinas and Bonaventura were Italian, Duns Scotus was Scottish, and Alexander Hales was English. The college system endorsed this cosmopolitanism. The student body was organized around four "nations"—France, Normandy, Picardy, and England—while the Danish, Swedish, Scottish, Navarre, and Lombard colleges were particularly well-known.

> "Anyone, whoever they are, wherever they come from, and whatever their religion, is free to teach medicine."
> Guillem VII, seigneur of Montpellier, in 1181

Universities provided fertile ground for the synthesis of redis-covered Greek (especially Aristotelian) ideas with more recent Christian thought. As early as the late 1100s, Montpellier was harboring Jewish and Arab scholars driven out of the Iberian peninsula by the *Reconquista*. Islamic scholars had not simply preserved these works of science and philosophy, but added to them in impressive ways. This was especially true for mathemat-ics—it was at this time that Arabic numerals started to infiltrate the west—as well as astronomy, astrology, and cartography. Tech-nologies such as windmills and water clocks traveled the same route, as did medicine. Medical faculties drew heavily on the works of Galen and other physicians from antiquity, but invari-ably through respected Arabic commentators such as Ibn Rushd

Ibn Sina, known as Avicenna in the West, became a staple of the syllabus in medieval medical faculties like Montpellier.

(Averroes), El-Razi (Rhazes), and Ibn Sina (Avicenna).

Learning and Power

As the Sorbonne cemented its reputation as Europe's premier university, its teachers began talking of a divinely ordained *translatio studii* ("transfer of learning") by which Paris claimed the intellectual mantle of Athens and Rome. Tellingly, this aligned conveniently with *translatio imperii* ("transfer of rule")—the idea that French kings were the legitimate heirs of ancient imperial authority. According to the Sorbonne's legal scholars, the authority of their royal patron derived not just from his status as feudal overlord but also from the classical notion that a king was emperor in his own kingdom (*rex in regni suo est imperator regni*). Since the ruler acted for the common good of his people, he could pass laws that applied across the whole of the realm, free from feudal mediation or interference. The title *rex Franciae* (king of France) began to be used in preference to the earlier *rex Francorum* (king of the Franks).

While adopting this more territorial conception of kingship, the monarchy also adapted its governing style to changes in French society. The royal household grew in size and became organized on a more rational basis, with a solid corps of state functionaries. State finances were set in order, complemented by a system of local tax officials. In 1307 the *Parlement de Paris*—France's premier court of law—was created, buttressed by the appointment of local judges (*baillis* and *sénéchaux*) in the provinces. There was also a national parliament, the Estates General, created in 1302, although it remained more of a consultative body that rubber-stamped royal policies than a platform for opposition. The king still shared power with the aristocratic elite. Even so, an enlarged bureaucracy and new urban and ecclesiastical institutions offered a strong challenge to the old feudal pyramid.

Vaulting Ambitions

The grand buildings that housed many of these new bodies had a highly distinctive appearance. By this point Gothic was all the rage across Europe. The origins of the architectural style

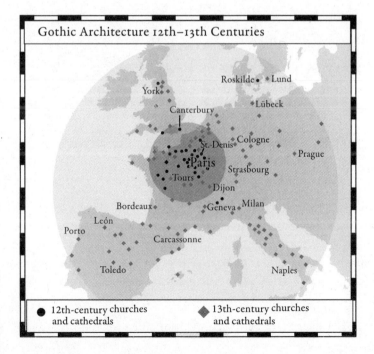

Gothic Architecture 12th–13th Centuries

York
Roskilde • Lund
Canterbury
Lübeck
St-Denis • Cologne
Paris
Prague
Tours
Strasbourg
Dijon
Bordeaux
Geneva • Milan
León
Porto
Carcassonne
Toledo
Naples

● 12th-century churches and cathedrals ◆ 13th-century churches and cathedrals

can be traced back to the Abbey of Saint-Denis, just north of Paris. From 1130, the Capetian propagandist-in-chief Abbé Suger had rebuilt the dynastic necropolis, making systematic use of a narrow, pointed arch instead of the rounded Romanesque one.

This officially approved Capetian style soon spread throughout the kingdom. The cathedral of Sens, on the border of Burgundy, completed in the 1170s, is normally considered the first "proper" Gothic cathedral but the Gothic motifs soon seemed to be everywhere, not least at Notre-Dame in Paris. Stone masons and craftsmen who worked on these French buildings found themselves in demand all over Europe. Over the next two centuries, scores of magnificent cathedrals in the style were built in England, Germany, Italy, and further afield.

The Gothic western façade of Notre-Dame cathedral (right), 1200–1250, echoes the distinctive geometric lines of earlier Islamic architecture (al-Aqmar mosque in Cairo, left, built in 1125–1126).

The new Gothic idiom, known by contemporaries as *opus Francigenum* ("Frankish style"), was a source of great prestige for the Capetian monarchy. Indeed, it is still widely viewed as one of western Christendom's signal cultural achievements. Yet medieval Gothic owed a substantial debt to Islamic architecture. Many of its salient features—not only the pointed arch but also trefoil designs, ribbed vaulting, stained glass, and rose windows—were widespread in the Islamic world, and had moved into Europe by osmosis through Spain, Sicily, and the Crusader states, or along trade and pilgrim routes. Beneath the divisive Crusader rhetoric, the cultural boundaries between east and west remained highly porous.

Pandemic Times

The circulation of goods, technology, and ideas between Orient and Occident acted as a dynamo of progress in the medieval period. But connectivity had its perils. Eastern traffic also delivered France's nemesis: the Black Death of 1348–1353, which broke

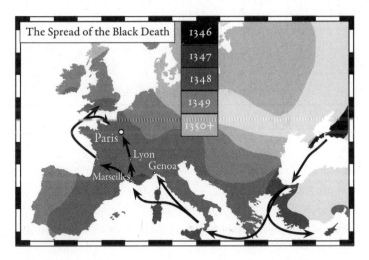

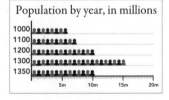

the back of European prosperity and cultural vigor.

Even in the wake of the global havoc caused by COVID-19, it is hard to grasp the scale of the impact—social, cultural, economic, and plain human—of the fourteenth-century plague. The overall crude mortality rate of the recent coronavirus pandemic has been estimated at less than one percent. By comparison, the Black Death caused the deaths of anywhere between a third and a half of the entire population of western Europe.

While the plague bacillus, *Yersinia pestis,* rightly gets the blame, it seems likely that climate change played a part in the pandemic's appearance. From the late thirteenth century, a cooling of average temperatures set in across much of the northern hemisphere, as the Warm Medieval Period segued into a Little Ice Age that would last until the nineteenth century. This climatic shift seems to coincide with the emergence of a virulent strain of the disease among burrowing rodents on the Eurasian steppe. Mutation allowed it to spread to fleas, which were carried by rats that stowed away in caravans traversing the great east-west Silk Road and on ships crossing the Black Sea and the Mediterranean.

A hecatomb rained down on humanity. Fourteenth-century science and medicine were simply not up to the task of understanding or treating this plague, the pneumonic form of which was especially lethal. Physicians had little to offer beyond advising people who lived near outbreaks to leave quickly, go far, and stay away as long as possible, unwittingly contributing to the disease's spread. Fear and ignorance bred a blame game: the Jews, or maybe lepers, must be poisoning Christian wells. Antisemitic pogroms and leper lynchings flared in the south and east of France particularly. The violence (though not the antisemitism) died down after 1351.

A peste, fame et bello libera nos, Domine
"From plague, famine and death deliver us, O Lord."
Late medieval prayer

The gruesome plague art of the period would develop into a full-blown danse macabre depicting individuals, high and low, being led to their deaths by grinning skeletons. Woodcuts of a now lost set of murals from the Cemetery of the Innocents in Paris, painted in the 1420s, gained widespread popularity for the black humor of the so-called Dance of Death.

The Black Death had a higher mortality than any other known pandemic in history. But it was far from a one-off. Severe outbreaks of the plague's less deadly, bubonic form—notably in 1360, 1369, and 1374—drastically slowed recovery. In most places the population did not reach pre-plague levels until after 1600. Indeed, bubonic plague remained a perennial threat: the last great outbreaks in France were in the 1630s, the 1660s, and in 1720–1721.

Plague was not the only scourge riding roughshod over four-teenth-century France. With the onset of the Little Ice Age, harvest failures became more common. A severe famine in 1315–1317 was followed by a major livestock epidemic. Food shortages were aggravated by war. The ruthless war-band armies of the period carried disease in their supply train—sometimes plague, but also influenza, typhus, smallpox, and other pathogens. Soldiers lived by plunder, seizing food and cattle from the beleaguered peasantry. Peasant revolts broke out, notably in Flanders in the 1320s and north of Paris in 1358.

Hard Times: The Jacquerie

Around Pentecost, in 1358, in the area to the north of Paris along the River Oise valley, a chronicler recorded that "a mysterious affliction" broke out, whereby "leaderless people gathered together, burned, and robbed everything and murdered gentlemen, noble ladies and their children; they raped ladies and virgins without any mercy whatsoever."

The Jacquerie was a response to the hardness of the times and the presumptions of the nobility, whose contemptuous name for the rebels, "Jacques" (from the type of padded tunic they wore, known as a *jacque*), gave the episode its name. The Jacquerie was put down with a savagery as shocking as any atrocity carried out during the revolt, which was the largest French peasant uprising until the Revolution of 1789.

One Hundred Years of Fortitude

War hit France especially hard in this period. From 1337 to 1453, the country was engaged in another epic conflict with England, which threatened its very existence as an independent state.

The *casus belli* of the Hundred Years' War was dynastic. The death of Charles IV without a direct male heir in 1328 marked the moment at which the proverbial luck of the Capetians ran out. Since French law stipulated royal inheritance through the male line, the crown passed to a cousin on the Valois branch, Philip VI. English tradition, by contrast, allowed female transmission of royal status, giving the Plantagenet kings (as the Angevin monarchs now styled themselves) a path to the throne. Edward III pressed his claim.

The long war that followed was a relentless game of chutes and ladders, with long truces alternating with intense periods of fighting and dramatic ascents and reversals of fortune. The conflict spread to other European countries—Spain, Portugal, Flanders, Wales, and Scotland—while in France it spawned internal conflicts as regional elites, notably in Brittany and Burgundy, jockeyed for power.

For some time, the English had the upper hand. They took early battle honors in brilliant victories at Crécy (1346) and Poitiers (1356). The Black Prince, son of Edward III, even managed to capture the French King John at Poitiers. The peace imposed on the French in 1361 at Brétigny, near Chartres, granted the English full control over most of southwestern France and also Calais and its environs.

England and France both struggled to stay at the top of the ladder. As the century wore on, the powerful dukes of Burgundy—a cadet branch of the Valois—entered the game. They sought to exploit the state's weakness during the long, distracted reign of Charles VI, whose delusions included the firm belief that he was made of glass. From 1407, Burgundians were effectively at war with Armagnacs, as supporters of the Valois were known. Both sought

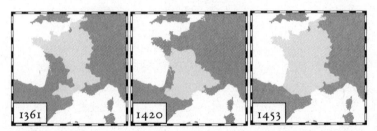

The changing fortunes of France: French territory between 1361 and 1453

alliance with England to strengthen their claims. In what was now a triangular conflict, the Burgundians profited from the stunning victory of the English king Henry V at Agincourt (1415), a humiliating bloodbath for the French nobility.

By stipulating Henry's marriage to Charles's daughter Catherine, the 1420 Treaty of Troyes envisioned a permanent union of France and England—and an end to the possibility of Valois rule. When both monarchs died in 1422, the English claimed the French throne for Henry V's infant son.

The English, together with the dukes of Burgundy, now ruled most of France north of the Loire. They occupied Paris, where in 1431 their new king, Henry VI, would be crowned in Notre-Dame cathedral just days after his tenth birthday. Yet the Anglo-French union and the Burgundian alliance were short-lived. Shakespeare may have burnished the exploits of the ruthless Henry V and his "band of brothers" as the stuff of English legend, but the period lingers in the French national memory due to the extraordinary figure of Joan of Arc.

The Maid of Orléans

"Jeanne d'Arc" probably never styled herself as such. She was better known in her lifetime as Joan "the Maiden" or Joan of Domrémy (her natal village) or Joan of Lorraine,

A contemporary drawing of Joan of Arc from 1429

after the imperial duchy in which it was situated. At birth, then, France's future patron saint had one foot in the Holy Roman Empire. Her charisma and spiritual conviction won over the Dauphin—the future Valois monarch Charles VII— forcing him out of a state of torpor to take the fight to the English. After helping Charles recapture Orléans in 1429, Joan led him to Reims to be crowned with full rites at the cathedral there. Yet despite helping to turn the tide of the conflict, Joan herself proved expendable. After she was captured by Burgundian forces and then handed over to the English, Charles VII did nothing to get her back. Joan was tried for heresy in an ecclesiastical court in Rouen and burned at the stake.

Despite her ignominious death, Joan's fabled exploits and military leadership helped to transform French fortunes. The Burgundians, sensing a reversal in the offing, abandoned the English for an alliance with the Valois kings. This wily change of tack gave the Valois the edge in the struggle against the English, who were driven out of Paris in 1436 and then back into the southwest. With defeat at Castillon near Bordeaux in 1453, the English lost all their French territories, save Calais. The French dynasty had finally disentangled itself from the English embrace.

The Last Battle

The 1453 battle of Castillon turned out to be the last major confrontation in the Hundred Years' War—though no one knew it at the time. It was also a preview of military things to come. Previously, artillery had been restricted to siege warfare. At Castillon, heavy cannon fire mustered by Charles VII's artillery commander, Jean Bureau, proved decisive against the English cavalry led by the legendary warrior Sir John Talbot. Mobile, wheeled cannons on the battlefield would forever change the conduct of war.

England was soon too distracted by the bloody Wars of the Roses (1455–1487) to consider re-entering the fray, but civil strife continued within France. The duchy of Brittany, which had taken advantage of the monarchy's weakness to become an autonomous state, was only brought back in line in 1488. Burgundy was an even bigger thorn in the Valois side: it took the death of Duke Charles the Bold in battle outside Nancy in 1477 to end the Burgundian challenge to royal sovereignty.

The dukes of Burgundy, scions of the Valois dynasty, were important players in the Anglo-French conflict. Through feats of arms, dynastic marriages, and diplomatic cunning, they built up a formidable slice of territory, including swaths of Flanders and the Low Countries, and seemed on the way to reviving Frankish Lotharingia as a buffer between France and the Holy Roman Empire. Charles the Bold's overweening ambitions alarmed his powerful neighbors, who breathed a collective sigh of relief on his death. After complex negotiations that lasted through the next decade, France and the Holy Roman Empire divided most of the duchy between themselves.

A New Confidence

France emerged from the Hundred Years' War and its aftermath battered but largely in one piece. The conflict had brought the French state to the brink of extinction, but by 1500 it was looking altogether stronger. The dynastic shift from Capetian to Valois had finally been settled, and the new ruling house had faced down formidable challenges to its authority, both foreign and domestic.

The economy had recovered much of the ground lost since the Black Death. Since 1439, the monarchy had enjoyed the right to impose on all subjects a national direct tax. This *taille* was granted by the Estates General on the condition it would be used specifically to pay for a standing army to drive the English out of France. As it turned out, this highly unpopular tax remained a staple of royal income until 1789.

The monarchy also retained the standing army. This was hugely significant. The conduct of warfare was changing drastically. Old-style wars between feudal levies of armored mounted knights and their archer vassals were fast becoming a thing of the past, swept aside by the arrival of gunpowder and cannon on the field of battle. Taxes had become the new sinews of war and the army an enforcer of the royal will, used against foreign enemies but also internally to repress dissent.

A new style of monarchy was emerging that was assertive, confident, and sure of its military prowess. In 1494, King Charles VIII proudly led an army into northern Italy with territorial expansion in mind, setting in motion the Italian Wars. Two years earlier, though, another event had occurred whose long-term impact would be far more historic: the arrival in 1492 of a Spanish vessel on the coastline of North America.

CHAPTER 3

NEW WORLDS

Exchange, Rebirth, and Reform (1500–1720)

Columbus's "discovery" of the Americas in 1492 was hardly a revelation to the sixty million people living there. But it certainly sparked astonishment in France and the rest of Europe. The realization that the Genoese navigator had stumbled across not the East Indies, as he first thought, but a quite unexpected continent raised a curtain on a new age of European exploration.

Over the next three centuries, a host of civilizations that had been perceived from Europe either dimly (China and India) or not at all (the Americas, Oceania, and, much later, Australasia) entered European consciousness. The jolt to old habits of mind was intense. Up to that point, the Atlantic had served as a liquid boundary to the old world. Now it was a door to new ones.

France Looks the Other Way

France proved slower than its European rivals to rise to the opportunities presented by the New World. In 1492, the young King Charles VIII had turned down a request from Columbus's brother to fund the epochal voyage. Two years later his priorities became clear as he launched a military campaign in north Italy and declared himself "King of Naples and Jerusalem." This sounded very much like a crusade to reestablish *France d'outremer*. Charles was reading from yesterday's script, looking eastward and backward when the rest of Europe was starting to look west—and to the future.

While France remained entangled in Italian wars until 1559, Spain and Portugal established huge global empires, as voyages of exploration transformed into exercises in crude but effective wealth extraction. The stupendous revenues from the gold and silver of the Americas funded fresh ventures. Vasco da Gama's rounding of the Cape of Good Hope in 1497 was a major step forward. He and his successors reached not only India but also the so-called Spice Islands of the Maluku peninsula, home to mace, nutmeg, and cloves. The port city of Manila in the Philippines, founded by Spain in 1571, developed as a key entrepôt, allowing the creation of a truly transglobal exchange of Mexican silver against Chinese silks, spices, porcelain, and other East Asian luxury products for European markets.

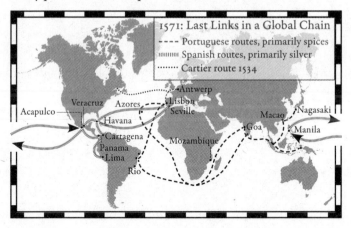

While the Iberian powers were busy grabbing the biggest prizes, France was otherwise engaged. It was more concerned with the decline in Silk Road traffic caused by the erosion of the Mongol empire and the growth of Ottoman power in the Mediterranean. When the French government finally dipped its toe into Atlantic waters in 1534, it was to commission the Breton seaman Jacques Cartier to look for a northwest passage that would give direct sea access to Asia. Cartier ended up establishing a colony near Quebec, the first European outpost in the far north of the continent since Viking Vinland. It lasted barely a year. Other early French attempts to found settlements there also failed, as did outposts in Florida and Brazil. (Present-day Quebec would only be founded in 1608.)

Montaigne and the Bon Sauvage

One of the earliest woodcuts of indigenous Americans to circulate in Europe: detail from *The Tupinambas of coastal Brazil at a cannibal feast*, Johann Froschauer, 1505

In 1550, some fifty individuals from the indigenous Tupinambá people from Brazil were shipped to Rouen to take part in a pageant before King Henry II. The philosopher Montaigne's encounter with the group on a later visit left him oscillating between stereotypes. On the one hand, the Tupinambás were widely thought to be cannibals, yet on the other, they seemed to retain a primeval purity worthy of "Nature's gentlemen." They had no vocabulary, Montaigne noted, for "lying, treachery, dissimulation, avarice, envy, detraction [and] pardon." His puzzlement betrays a durable view of non-Europeans as either bloodthirsty pagans or exotic exemplars of the noble savage. The Tupinambás are remembered in the French language in a name—*topinambour*—for the Jerusalem artichoke, though this humble tuber had been brought back to France from Canada and not the Brazilian tropics (or the Holy Land for that matter).

It seemed France was destined to miss out on New World bounty. Yet novelties of flora and fauna—and language—began to filter in from the Americas, including tomatoes, peanuts, avocados, pepper, and cacao, as well as staples such as maize, potatoes, manioc, and cassava. In 1560, the diplomat Jean Nicot—after whom nicotine was named—sent back to the royal court a sample of tobacco, with the recommendation that it be snorted as a medical remedy. In return, the Old World shipped to the new one a veritable Noah's Ark of fauna, ranging from horses, cows, goats and pigs to many species of earthworm.

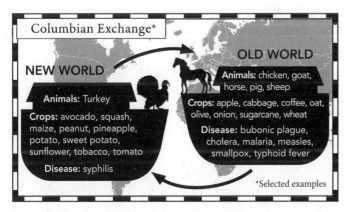

Columbian Exchange*

OLD WORLD

NEW WORLD

Animals: chicken, goat, horse, pig, sheep

Animals: Turkey

Crops: apple, cabbage, coffee, oat, olive, onion, sugarcane, wheat

Crops: avocado, squash, maize, peanut, pineapple, potato, sweet potato, sunflower, tobacco, tomato

Disease: bubonic plague, cholera, malaria, measles, smallpox, typhoid fever

Disease: syphilis

*Selected examples

Pathogens also hitched a ride on their human or animal hosts. During their siege of Naples in 1494–1495, Charles VIII's troops fell victim to a new disease that they called "*le mal napolitain.*" This "Neapolitan itch" was a version of syphilis, which the Americas had gifted Europe from frisky sailors on Columbus's ships. Yet this malady was small potatoes when set against the impact of Eurasian strains of smallpox, typhus, measles, whooping cough, chicken pox, and influenza. "Virgin-soil epidemics" devastated an indigenous population that lacked immunity to these diseases. The total die-off in the Americas from disease or related causes was around 90 percent, from a population of around sixty million in 1492 to barely six million in 1650. It was a far greater catastrophe for the American continent than the Black Death had been for Europe.

This largely unwitting exercise in biological ethnic cleansing had profound global consequences. Farming virtually ceased across much of the American continent. The regrowth of forest and bushland triggered a huge carbon uptake that cooled the world's climate. This was at a time when Europe was entering a particularly severe phase of its "Little Ice Age," linked to intense volcanic activity in Iceland, Japan, and the Philippines between 1637 and 1646. Across the seventeenth century, winters were harsher, summers cooler and droughts and floods multiplied. France was slow to benefit from early globalization, but there was nowhere to hide from its ecological effects.

Italian Infatuation

The nineteenth-century writer Jules Michelet once remarked that France gained less from these voyages of global discovery than from its "discovery" of Italy. During the Italian campaigns of 1494–1559, Charles VIII and his successors were deeply impressed by the achievements of this financial and cultural powerhouse. The

Italian states contained Europe's most advanced economies, its wealthiest and most beautiful cities, and its most refined princely courts, palaces, and villas. Set amid the ruins of antiquity, these new social nerve centers displayed a born-again commitment to classical tastes and values. For Italy was the home of the Renaissance and a cradle of humanism.

Renaissance Humanism

The Renaissance or rebirth of Western learning was grounded in a form of textual scholarship known as humanism. Since the demise of the Roman empire, scholars had looked to the works of classical Greece and Rome for inspiration. The appearance of new waves of manuscripts, many passed on from the Islamic world, revived this spirit of inquiry. Classical writers changed the ways that Europeans thought about everything. Humanists sought from ancient texts the keys to understanding what it meant to be human, as well as ways to make the world a more civilized place.

Two works published in 1543 challenged centuries of assumptions about humanity's place in the cosmos. *On the Revolutions of the Celestial World* by the Polish astronomer Copernicus showed that the Earth revolved around the Sun rather than the other way around, opening up unthought-of dimensions of outer space. In his illustrated work *On the Fabric of the Human Body*, the Flemish anatomist Vesalius, a former medical student at the University of Paris, offered a detailed dissection of the inner space of human anatomy.

Both men spent time on the Italian peninsula, where they studied the texts of antiquity through a humanist lens. They

Macrocosm and microcosm: The explorations of Copernicus (left) and Vesalius (right) revolutionized our understanding of humans and their place in the universe.

were not content with merely emulating the learning of the ancients; they strove to surpass it, braving the disapproval of the church along the way. Copernicus's new cosmology owed much to his close observation of the heavenly bodies. Vesalius's anatomical insights were grounded in the evidence of his own extraordinary eye, trained in meticulous dissections of human cadavers.

The impact of this new thinking on France owes much to a third foreigner, the Strasbourg-based printer Johann Gutenberg. His experiments with moveable type and printing presses had sparked a print revolution that guaranteed the humanists a large and avid audience across Europe. The Sorbonne founded a printing press in Paris in 1470 and the first printed book in French was published in Lyon six years later. Just under three thousand books were published in France by 1500, a figure that soared to seventy-five thousand in the sixteenth century and grew exponentially thereafter.

Print was the dynamite in an intellectual time bomb. Italian humanists, often sponsored by wealthy patrons, explored a wider field of inquiry than universities. They ranged through science and philosophy to art, architecture, poetry, music, and literature—not to mention *savoir vivre*. At Italian princely courts, new standards of social conduct refined or replaced those of knightly chivalry. The quintessential humanist conduct book, Castiglione's much-imitated *The Courtier*, was translated into French in 1537 and formed the basis of gentlemanly rules of etiquette at the royal court until the French Revolution.

> Practise in everything a certain nonchalance that shall conceal design and show that what is done and said is done without effort and almost without thought.
> From *The Courtier* by Baldassare Castiglione

French monarchs set about importing Italian culture wholesale, both in the form of material works of art and the artists themselves. As French architects and stonemasons had once spread Gothic architecture to the rest of Europe, so, too, Italian painters, sculptors, architects, craftsmen, cooks, garden designers, and intellectuals now took the road north. The writings of the great Roman architectural theorist Vitruvius were translated into French in 1547. The Gothic style was soon passé, swept aside by a revived classical aesthetic.

Paris was a prime mover of this cultural appropriation, though big southern cities such as Lyon housed colonies of Italian writers and craftsmen. Many of the chateaux of the Loire Valley were built, remodelled or decorated in the Italian style. Andrea del Sarto, Leonardo da Vinci—who died in Amboise in 1519—and Benvenuto Cellini were only the most famous of those lured to France. Francis I (1515–1547) was a particularly keen importer of

Italian masters to instruct their French counterparts on the latest styles. In 1530 he established the "School of Fontainebleau" to decorate the royal palace there and diffuse Renaissance ideals and techniques across France.

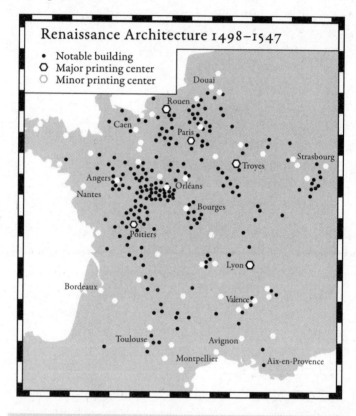

Renaissance Architecture 1498–1547

- • Notable building
- ◉ Major printing center
- ○ Minor printing center

Douai
Rouen
Caen
Paris
Strasbourg
Troyes
Angers
Nantes
Orléans
Bourges
Poitiers
Lyon
Bordeaux
Valence
Toulouse
Avignon
Montpellier
Aix-en-Provence

The Mother Tongue

In 1530, Francis I set up the *Collège du Roi* (now *Collège de France*) as a bastion of humanist scholarship in Paris. Unlike the Sorbonne, where Latin held sway, the royal institute taught Hebrew and Greek from the outset. The

French language was, moreover, on the move. The royal edict of Villers-Cotterêts in 1539 ordered the use of the "French maternal language" in all official documents. The retirement of Latin from public life was hastened by the emergence of outstanding writers in the vernacular such as Rabelais, Montaigne, Ronsard, and Marguerite de Navarre, the king's sister.

The cultural spoils of the Italian Renaissance were some consolation for France's meager territorial gains in Italy. The campaigns had begun with high hopes. Charles VIII's army of close to thirty thousand men was huge even by contemporary standards—Cortez had triumphed over the Aztec empire with only six hundred fighting men. Many of the troops were expensive Swiss and German foreign mercenaries, but Charles could afford to pay them because of taxation rights enjoyed by the French crown since 1439. War had become the sport of kings. Few others could afford it.

The Italian campaigns had their high and low points. French artillery had the tall but thin Italian city fortifications toppling like ninepins in the 1490s. Brilliant battlefield victories such as Fornovo (1495) and Marignano (1515) would follow. But so, too, did epic defeats such as Pavia, where in 1525 Francis I was taken prisoner. Ultimately, a disproportionate amount of time, money, and human life was spent for not very much.

The Eastern Frontier Shapes Up
The treaty of Cateau-Cambrésis in 1559 that ended the Italian Wars closed some doors and opened others. On the one hand, France renounced all claims on territory

in Italy and the Low Countries. On the other, England finally ceded Calais, its last toehold on the continent. Also important was France's acquisition of the *Trois Évêchés* ("Three Bishoprics") of Toul, Metz, and Verdun in the northeast. The river Rhône had once marked France's southeastern frontier. That border had crept eastward with the incorporation of Dauphiné in the fourteenth century and Provence in the fifteenth, along with gains in Burgundy following Charles the Bold's death, in 1477. Now the acquisition of the *Trois-Évêchés* reinforced this drift and firmed up the eastern edges of the Hexagon.

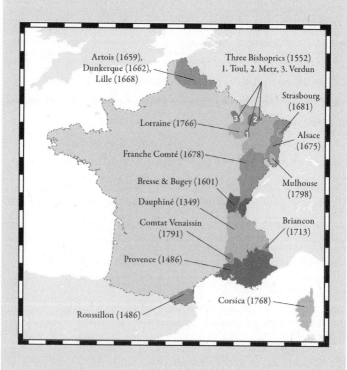

Artois (1659), Dunkerque (1662), Lille (1668)

Three Bishoprics (1552) 1. Toul, 2. Metz, 3. Verdun

Strasbourg (1681)

Lorraine (1766)

Alsace (1675)

Franche Comté (1678)

Bresse & Bugey (1601)

Mulhouse (1798)

Dauphiné (1349)

Briancon (1713)

Comtat Venaissin (1791)

Provence (1486)

Corsica (1768)

Roussillon (1486)

Wars of Faith and Fury

At the height of the Italian Wars, on October 31, 1517, the German priest and theologian Martin Luther nailed his Ninety-five Theses to the door of the Schlosskirche in Wittenberg, challenging the authority of the church in Rome and sparking a religious reformation that would engulf much of Europe. Unlike other Christian humanists such as Erasmus, who thought flaws could be remedied by internal reform, Luther decided the only solution was a complete break from an institution he came to believe was headed by a papal Antichrist. In the Peasant War of 1525, the strife that followed his challenge ripped through German lands and parts of present-day eastern France. Later in the century, all of France was sucked into the maelstrom of its own religious wars.

The new medium of print fanned the flames of religious conflict. Huge numbers of pamphlets circulated in French with crude and provocative woodcuts aimed at a largely illiterate audience. Print was a double-edged sword: it could promote religious solidarity, but it also bitterly polarized communities. Small groups of Protestant "reformers" (or Huguenots, as they were somewhat mysteriously called) formed throughout France from the 1520s. In 1534, salacious printed posters *(placards)* denouncing the Catholic mass appeared around Paris, injecting a new level of venom. The Placards Affair triggered repressive state action—including heresy trials and burnings—to discourage would-be recruits to the Protestant cause.

Travel in the Lands of Fantasy

The role of print in Europe's intellectual development is often painted in rosy colors. Certainly it diffused scientific discoveries, great literature, and objective truth—but

also, as the Reformation showed, prejudice, error, and incitement to violence. The popular genre of travel literature is a case in point. Some works faithfully described new lands and peoples encountered by explorers, but others peddled old myths, fantasies and prejudices. One of the most widely circulated travelogues—rivalling in popularity the travels in China of Venetian merchant Marco Polo—was the memoir of "Sir John Mandeville," purportedly an English knight writing in French. First printed in 1480, its avowedly authentic portrayals of far-off lands featured descriptions of wool-growing trees, gold-digging ants, two-headed geese, headless humans, and people with only one giant foot, sixty-foot cannibals, and sundry other monsters. Columbus himself took along a copy on his 1492 voyage.

Luther's fellow humanist Jean Calvin, born in Noyon in Picardy, played a vital role in spreading Protestant ideas throughout Europe, albeit from outside French borders. In the 1530s he fled persecution as a heretic and settled in the independent city-state of Geneva. There he created the spiritual headquarters of Protestantism, trained a new priesthood, sent out missionaries, and provided the scattered community with a sense of unity. By 1560, French Protestants numbered around two million, roughly 10 percent of the population.

Dealing with this social discontent was made all the more difficult by the economic turbulence caused by the discovery of the New World. The influx of silver and gold from the Americas meant a torrential rise in money supply that inevitably triggered inflation at unheard-of levels. The price of commodities soared five-fold across Europe over the century. As state spending soared, governments found themselves struggling to stay solvent, a dilemma they tried to resolve by debasing their currencies. France managed five such devaluations in the 1560s and 1570s alone.

Fresh injections of silver from Mexico and Peru did, however, stimulate French industry—albeit somewhat circuitously. Rather than invest in their own businesses, the Spanish sought out financial services and manufactured goods from northwestern Europe, notably the Low Countries, England, and northern France. Spanish silver set French towns to work, fueling an urban boom that generated even greater wealth.

At the top, a sizeable merchant class was now committed heavily to foreign trade and private means of production. This mercantile order challenged the traditional social hierarchy topped by the nobility and grounded in land ownership. Nobles reacted more or less well to the development, some becoming commercially minded, others sinking into mediocrity and debt. Medieval feudalism was in decay and capitalism on the march. Yet these shifts produced huge problems at the bottom of the social ladder. Wages chased prices upward across the sixteenth century, but as the population was growing even more rapidly, the purchasing power of most people fell. Beggars and wandering vagrants became a common sight across France, prompting anxious urban elites to experiment with new poor laws and draconian policing schemes.

The monarchy was not in a good place for dealing with these fermenting tensions. The death of Henry II in a jousting accident in 1559 left his widow, Catherine de' Medici, as regent to his successors, the brothers Francis II, Charles IX, and Henry III, as they would become. The crown's weakness and Catherine's vacillations would be a baleful influence on government once the Wars of Religion (1562–1598) got under way.

Religion split the old ruling elite in two. High-ranking Catholic nobility such as the Guise dynasty from eastern France had returned from the Italian Wars fired with a new religious zeal. They put pressure on the monarchy to adopt strong anti-Calvinist measures. On the Protestant side, the Bourbons (based in southwestern France) and the Coligny family (from the east) played similar roles. Factions stirred up religious violence only to exploit it in attempts to wrest power from the monarchy. Foreign regimes piled on the pressure. Spain egged on the Catholic cause, while the newly formed Dutch Republic or "United Provinces" (the present-day Netherlands) looked to create a cross-border Protestant Internationale.

St. Bartholomew's Day Massacre

The low point in the Wars of Religion and the nadir of

the regency was the infamous St. Bartholomew's Day massacre in Paris in 1572. Catherine's decision to marry her daughter Marguerite to the Protestant prince Henry of Navarre scandalized Catholic opinion. The vehemently anti-Huguenot city of Paris hosted the marriage, which was attended by leading Protestant lights, including their leader, Admiral Gaspard de Coligny. It seems Catherine and the young monarch Charles IX ordered their assassination shortly afterward. With the bell of the church of Saint-Germain-l'Auxerrois near the Louvre tolling a warning, armed gangs of Catholics combed the streets on a killing spree. At least three thousand Protestants died in Paris, possibly many more: people were picking corpses out of the Seine as far downriver as Le Havre in the weeks that followed. Thousands more died in similar massacres in the provinces.

Detail from *Le Massacre de la Saint Barthélemy* by François Dubois, showing the murder of Coligny

By drawing a line of blood between the two religious communities, the St. Bartholomew's Day Massacre radicalized politics in a way that made France almost ungovernable. It did not help that the authority of Henry III, who acceded to the crown in 1574, was undermined by the childlessness of his marriage and his preference for same-sex partners. The death in 1584 of his younger brother threatened the extinction of the Valois line when Henry died. The law seemed to dictate that the throne should pass to the Bourbon line in the person of another Henry, ruler of the small Basque kingdom of Navarre in the western Pyrenees. But Henry of Navarre was a Protestant. This set Catholic alarm bells ringing.

The dynastic endgame to the wars proved extraordinarily fraught and violent. The Guises sponsored the formation in Paris of a radical Catholic League, which fomented populist anti-Huguenot violence. The king's decision in 1588 to order the assassination of the Guise faction leaders drove both sides to extremes. In 1589, following his alliance with Henry of Navarre, Henry III was himself assassinated by a fanatical Catholic monk.

New Dynasty, False Dawn

With Henry of Navarre's assumption of the throne as Henry IV, first ruler of the Bourbon dynasty, the fighting intensified. Paris and other large cities held out doggedly against the new Protestant king. But the French capital was, Henry famously declared, "well worth a mass." In 1593, he converted to Catholicism, neatly squaring the politico-religious circle.

This sudden change of tack pulled the rug from under the feet of his Catholic opponents. And in 1598, his politically deft Edict of Nantes won over any Protestant doubters by granting them official toleration, plus a degree of political autonomy in their heartlands. In the same year, he made peace with Spain, which had been exploiting the religious turmoil for years.

The Edict of Nantes seemed to turn a page for the French monarchy and its people. The new king trumped his childless Valois predecessor in 1601 by producing a son and heir, the future Louis XIII. To his reputation as peacemaker he added policies that aimed to restore prosperity, promising to "put a chicken in every pot." Henry's Protestant minister, Sully, stabilized the royal finances and took steps to promote agriculture and boost industry through public works.

POVRTRAIT DE LA STATVE EQVESTRE
Esleué a Paris sur le Pont-Neuf pour la glorieuse memoire de HENRY LE
GRAND Roy de France et de Nauarre
RESTAVRATEVR DE LA LIBERTE FRANCOISE

Henry IV's statue, erected on the Pont Neuf in Paris in 1614, became a site of veneration for this most genuinely popular of monarchs.

Henry bestowed special favor on Paris, which had contained his most vehement enemies in the 1590s. He sponsored new building at the Louvre and Tuileries palaces, founded what became the Gobelins tapestry works, completed the Pont Neuf, the first bridge to span the whole of the Seine, and constructed the Place des Vosges—the first planned square in France—as part of an unfinished project to stimulate silk weaving in the east of the city.

Yet Henry IV's reign proved a false dawn. The king not only failed to quench the fires of religious dissent, he fell victim to them. In 1610, when stuck in his carriage in the middle of a Parisian traffic jam, he was assassinated by a radical monk, just as his predecessor had been. The deadly cocktail of religious intolerance and ruthless factional politics still had some way to run.

Counter-Reformation

By now the Catholic Church was strategically fighting against the Reformation. Since the Council of Trent (1545–1563), the papacy had pursued a variety of reforms to remedy abuses within the church, before taking the fight to Protestant territory. Even as the Wars of Religion subsided, a new and zealously committed Catholic clergy emerged, professionally trained in diocesan seminaries and primed to promote Tridentine reforms. They were joined by a myriad of new religious orders, some of them imports from Italy (Jesuits, Oratorians) or Spain (Carmelites, Brothers of Charity), others homegrown, such as Vincent de Paul's Lazarists and the Daughters of Charity.

Louise de Marillac and the Daughters of Charity

A striking feature of this French "age of saints" was the scale of women's involvement, coupled with an emphasis on teaching and charitable work that reached all levels of society. In 1635, Louise de Marillac co-founded with Vincent de Paul the Daughters (or Sisters) of Charity, France's most important and very soon its largest female religious community. Its commitment to nursing and educating the sick poor was much admired and widely copied. Vincent was canonized in 1737, Louise in 1934. The fact that she was illegitimate delayed her recognition for centuries, though the canonization in 1929 of Joan of Arc, another woman who defied the gender roles of her time, may have helped to revive her cause.

The Counter-Reformation left its mark on French cities. A heroic age of ecclesiastical building and rebuilding after bouts of Protestant iconoclasm ensued. In Paris alone perhaps a hundred churches were built or substantially reworked. It was at this time that the dome became a prominent feature of urban skyscapes, popularized by St. Peter's Basilica in Rome, completed in 1626. Val-de-Grâce in the 1640s was the first example in Paris; many others followed. As Louis XIII bestowed favor on the Catholic renewal, these new-look cities became a hostile environment for Protestants.

Missionaries trained in the arts of preaching against heresy and ignorance also carried the Catholic message overseas, notably to areas where France was expanding its commercial or military presence. One such pioneer was François Xavier, a founding member of the Society of Jesus, who reached as far as India, China, and Japan in the 1540s. By the seventeenth century, the Jesuits had turned these early forays into a global mission, diffusing not only the precepts of Rome but also architectural and artistic styles associated with it.

Raison d'État

Louis XIII was only eight when he came to the throne in 1610. Power passed into the hands of his widowed mother, Marie de'

Medici, who became regent. Though not related to Catherine de' Medici, she was just as unpopular, as was her Italian chief adviser Concino Concini.

In 1617, the teenage Louis had Concini assassinated and banished his mother from court. Marie remained a brooding presence in court politics for over two decades, contributing to a general air of instability that was aggravated by Louis's failure for many years to produce an heir. The birth in 1638 of the child who would become Louis XIV—after more than twenty years of marriage to Anne of Austria—was widely viewed as a miracle. It calmed but did not entirely dispel succession anxieties. There was trouble brewing in the east, too, in the form of the Thirty Years' War (1618–1648), one of the bloodiest conflicts in European history that would eventually draw in all major powers on the continent.

These years witnessed a tectonic shift in French government policy. In time, this would lead to a strengthened monarchy emerging at the head of a centralized state. The masterminds of this enterprise were two Cardinal Ministers: Richelieu, chief minister to the king, and his Italian protégé Mazarin (Giulio Mazzarini), royal adviser from Richelieu's death in 1642 until his own in 1660.

Raison d'état was Cardinal Richelieu's raison d'être. Above any moral or religious considerations, the interests of the state always came first and last. He shared the opinion of the jurist Jean Bodin that "the king is responsible only to God and his conscience"—an approach that would come to define the dynasty's sense of itself as not only divinely appointed but also above the human laws of the land. The king would be expected to respect tradition, but was in essence an "absolute" ruler—and France as a whole was embodied in him. In other words, the interests of the state and the interests of the king were one and the same.

One of Richelieu's first steps toward forging an absolute monarchy was to cleanse the royal council of rebellious magnates, replacing them with clients he regarded as trustworthy, industrious, and competent. The Intendants, as these state officials were known, were given wide-ranging powers in the provinces to impose royal policies and collect taxes. Any aristocrat who questioned this royal prerogative risked severe punishment, as François de Montmorency-Bouteville discovered to his cost in 1627: the scion of one of France's most ancient ducal dynasties was ceremonially decapitated in the heart of Paris for daring to fight a duel against Richelieu's express wishes.

Richelieu squeezed out consultative or representative bodies. Before 1614, the national parliament—the Estates General—had often been called to help find solutions to religious and other troubles. Richelieu refused to convene it and was similarly dismissive of provincial assemblies. Of the major provinces, only Brittany, Burgundy, and Languedoc were allowed fully functioning estates.

Pamphleteers attacked Richelieu as a ruthless, Machiavellian schemer. The Cardinal took the flak in stride, but he built a fierce system of state censorship all the same. It was on his watch that *lettres de cachet* (royal detention orders) and the Bastille prison acquired their notoriety. He stamped out any hint of dissent in the provinces caused by his tax policies. Yet he also understood that repression was not enough to win hearts and minds, and he brought together a team of state propagandists to pitch the government's policies to the public. In 1640, he founded the *Imprimerie royale,* the royal printworks, and tasked it with "multiplying good books that serve the king's glory." Richelieu strove diligently to get intellectuals on the monarchy's side.

Théophraste Renaudot and the Gazette

The maverick physician and philanthropist Théophraste Renaudot was France's first journalist and news editor. Crude news-sheets carrying market information and government decrees had circulated throughout Europe in the Renaissance, often written by hand. Under Richelieu's tutelage, Renaudot embraced the medium of print. Founded in 1631, the *Gazette* was designed, he confessed in an early issue, to be "the journal of kings and of the powers of the earth." Its establishment tone persisted well into the eighteenth century, when it faced stiff competition from rival, less stuffy newspapers. Famously, *La Gazette* did not report the storming of the Bastille in July 1789.

Strengthening the state domestically helped to improve its international position. As the Thirty Years' War played out, Habsburg Spain and Austria threatened France with encirclement. Richelieu's view that this should be stopped at any cost brought him into conflict with Catholic hardliners, or *dévots,* who regarded the crushing of Protestantism as the primordial duty of state. On the "Day of the Dupes" in 1630, a *dévot*

conspiracy almost succeeded in deposing Richelieu, who was saved only when the king belatedly rallied to his support. The Cardinal's opponents were crushed, but their critique of royal policy would resurface in later times of crisis.

Given the instability of the French state, Richelieu resisted pitching into the Thirty Years' War too early. Instead, he chose an oblique approach, providing financial subsidies to enemies of the Habsburgs, including Protestant powers such as Sweden and the Dutch Republic. By 1635, the Cardinal believed France was ready for open war. Yet no sooner had it engaged than disaster loomed: Spanish forces seized the frontier fortress at Corbie near Amiens in 1636, leaving open the road to Paris. Richelieu and Louis XIII in person mustered a force that retook Corbie, ending the invasion panic.

Keeping the ship of state afloat involved much bigger armies, while Richelieu also became fixated on building a navy. A massive recruitment drive bolstered army numbers from 20,000 to more than 150,000 by the end of the 1630s. Along with technological advances in firearms, cannon, and fortifications, this made war hideously expensive. With France openly engaged in war, taxes rained down on a population already struggling with endemic food shortages and sometimes outright famine. Bubonic plague was still chronic: the 1628–1631 outbreak was particularly devastating, killing up to a million people.

These were tough times to raise taxes. But the war had to be paid for. France's main direct tax, the *taille* (from which the nobility was largely exempt), and the indirect salt tax, the *gabelle,* both doubled in the years leading up to 1635. In the popular imagination, the royal tax collector grew into a kind of fifth horseman of the Apocalypse. Tax revolts became endemic, and some protests—the Croquants in 1624 and 1637 in the southwest, for example, and the Va-Nu-Pieds in Normandy in 1636—reached menacing proportions.

The Cardinal's Inheritance

Domestic rebellion did not end with the death of either Richelieu in 1642 or Louis XIII a year later. Their successors—Cardinal Mazarin and Anne of Austria, regent to the four-year-old Louis XIV— doubled down on Richelieu's policies. Their survival in power was particularly impressive given the period of intense internal rebellion across France known as the Fronde (1648–1652), in which the entire political elite was swept along in a fast-moving drama with as many shifts in fortune as a Molière farce.

March of the Catapults

A *fronde* is a child's catapult, and there was much about the rebellion that seemed schoolboyish—or school-girlish, for many of the most prominent *frondeurs* were women. At one stage when Paris was being besieged by royal forces, the *frondeuse* Duchess de Montpensier, daughter of the duke of Orléans, trained the defenders' cannon on the person of the king. Ultimately, the Fronde proved to be the last throw of the dice by the old aristocracy to stop the development of absolute monarchy. It has been argued that the rebellion was too frivolous to succeed. Yet its impact on the wider population was anything but: armed mercenaries pillaged whole areas during the frequent breakdowns in public order. Population losses in the Ile de France from famine, disease, and warfare approached the scale of the Black Death.

In the immediate aftermath of the Fronde, Gaston, Duke of Orléans, casually informed his daughter that "the monarchy is finished; it cannot survive in its present state." In retrospect, it seems astonishing that the monarchy was able to survive intact, let alone embark on one of the most brilliant eras of its history. Though widely scapegoated for the kingdom's ills, Cardinal Mazarin enjoyed a victory that was a triumph for the model of centralized government mapped out by Richelieu.

Reign of the Sun King

After the death of Mazarin in 1661, Louis XIV made one small but highly significant adjustment to the template devised by the cardinals. The twenty-two-year-old took on full power in his own right. From now on, the king would rule without a first minister, while any opposition to royal policy was now tinged with treason.

The young monarch had no intention of being a shrinking violet, especially not in international affairs. He ardently desired *la gloire* and happily accepted the sobriquet "Louis le Grand" (Louis the Great) after only modest success in the War of Devolution (1667–1668). Thankfully his run of military luck continued. The Dutch War (1672–1678) and War of the Reunions (1679–1684) saw France make appreciable gains in Flanders and Alsace, while also managing to incorporate Burgundian Franche-Comté, previously in Spanish hands.

L'état, c'est moi

Louis XIV almost certainly never uttered the historic catchphrase we associate with him. Yet it neatly expresses his firm conviction that sovereignty, by divine fiat, was embodied in his physical frame. The king's obsession

Louis XIV: bust by Bernini, 1665

with his own grandeur would reach epic proportions. No western ruler since the Roman emperor Augustus had so many images of himself produced, nor in such an array of media: print, paint, bronze, stone, tapestry, pastel, enamel, wood, terracotta, and wax. Invariably, Louis posed in the grand manner, with more or less implicit references to great figures from the past such as Alexander the Great, Augustus, or Charlemagne, and even the gods of antiquity.

Global Glory and Gold

In addition to his quest for glory in Europe, Louis also sought to achieve a global presence. This involved a lengthy game of catch-up with his international rivals.

Louis's predecessors had already marked out the main strategies to follow. Henry IV's approach had been to copy the Dutch, considering them the most successful at pressing home their trade advantages and overseas presence. While Spain was running a huge balance-of-payments deficit and teetering on the brink of bankruptcy, the tiny new Dutch Republic was rapidly turning into the wealthiest state in Europe. This owed much to the chartered trading company model, which the Dutch and English pioneered. Under this system, cartels of private investors were granted exclusive state-backed privileges in certain areas of global trade. The model fit into a general economic system whose watchwords were boosting exports, reducing imports, and trading in global markets. This formula, later described as mercantilism, was the recipe for greatness that France would learn to cook by.

Louis XIV made chartered companies a central plank of royal policy, buttressed by a much strengthened navy that could protect French merchants overseas, as Richelieu had been the first to grasp. In all these policy matters, Louis was advised by Jean-Baptiste Colbert. A protégé of Mazarin from a merchant background, Colbert had insinuated himself into the royal entourage through sheer intellect and industry, becoming an all-purpose ministerial factotum from 1661 until his death two decades later. Adopting the chartered company model with enthusiasm, in 1664 he established a West Indies company based in Le Havre, as well as an East Indies company in the newly built seaport of Lorient in Brittany. He went on to use similar bodies to explore trading possibilities in Senegal, the main area from which Africans were exported as slaves to Caribbean and American plantations.

Richelieu had already established a presence in the Caribbean at Saint Kitts, Martinique, and Guadeloupe, with an eye to developing tobacco and sugar plantations on the English model. In 1664, Colbert brought the former pirate haunt of Saint-Domingue, present-day Haiti, under French control and turned it to sugar production. Sugar and tobacco were addictive commodities with global appeal, and the reliance of their plantations on the slave trade gave Colbert no qualms: *raison d'état oblige. . . .* Indeed, he drafted the infamous *Code noir* that regulated slavery in French colonies. As it was promulgated two years after his death, the minister would not live to see the vast wealth the Caribbean islands would generate, nor the extraordinary human misery his Black Code engendered.

The Black Code

The first recommendations of the 1685 ordinance were to exclude Protestants and Jews from the colonies, in keeping with Louis XIV's growing religious intolerance at the time. Yet its regulations for the slave trade were for the long haul. Indeed, the *Code noir* would not be fully repealed until 1848. There are few traces of humanity in the document. Owners were directed to educate and care for the soul and body of their slaves and not force them to work on Sundays. But these concessions pale beside the stark cruelty ordained for all other aspects of slaves' lives, including their capture and sale, with the threat of severe corporal and even capital punishment for stepping out of line.

Success in foreign markets also required stronger industries at home. Colbert believed that boosting exports and cutting imports, particularly of expensive manufactured goods, would steadily improve France's finances. Henry IV had pioneered this approach. His creation of the Gobelins factory in Paris was designed to sate the hunger of the wealthy elite for fine Flemish-style carpets. It had the added bonus of encouraging foreigners to buy French, thus attracting foreign bullion and undermining competitors.

Colbert embraced this top-down, dirigiste approach. On his watch, national prosperity would be grounded in the state's creative intervention in the economy. Besides the Gobelins, he also offered state support for the manufacture of tapestries in Beauvais, carpets at La Savonnerie in the Paris suburbs, mirrors at Saint-Gobain, and cheap knockoffs of coveted Japanese and Chinese porcelain at Saint-Cloud. These policies were combined with aggressive tariffs aimed at keeping foreign competitors at bay.

The Two Faces of the Grand Siècle

Not all of Colbert's many economic initiatives paid off. The state was notoriously neglectful of agriculture, which employed more than three quarters of French men and women and yet had been in the doldrums for some time. Even so, the economy was in decent shape at the time of his death in 1683. Following the pioneering examples of the Dutch and English, Colbert had helped to build up France into a commercial and industrial power with global reach, while his dirigiste pathway for development–"Colbertism"–left a trail for future policymakers to follow. Indeed, the 1680s proved to be the apogee of Louis XIV's reign. France's status as a global player had been established, while the king's victorious wars in search of glory and grandeur made France, a panegyrist wrote, what Spain had been a century beforehand, "the terror of Europe."

Yet for Louis, greatness lay not just on the battlefield but also in the cultural sphere. Indeed, showy initiatives were a form of soft power that complemented his military prowess. As absolute ruler by divine right, Louis expected to be obeyed within France. But he also sought to persuade, seduce, charm, and, if possible, astonish elites across Europe with his country's cultural superiority. Louis's apologists until the Revolution of 1789 and beyond would extol his role in creating the "Grand Siècle" (the Great Century).

One cornerstone of royal cultural policies under Louis was the academy of scholars, scientists, and men of letters. The early model here was *l'Académie française*, founded in 1635 by Richelieu to promote the use of the French language as a vehicle for clear expression. In addition, the Academy of Painting and Sculpture (1648) was established as an official arbiter of artistic taste and best practice. These royal bodies were soon joined by academies of Dance (1661), Inscriptions and Belles-Lettres (1663), Sciences (1666), Architecture (1671), and Music (1672).

The creation of a French Academy in Rome in 1666 testified to a continuing fascination with the Italian fine arts and classical heritage. Yet a telling moment occurred in 1671 when, having summoned Gian Lorenzo Bernini, the greatest artist of the age, to design a new east façade for the Louvre palace in Paris, Louis rejected the Italian's plans and sent him packing back to Rome. Encouraged by his scientific adviser Charles Perrault (of fairy-tale fame), Louis turned instead to Charles's architect brother Claude for the project. The message was clear: when it came to culture, the French were now better than the best in the rest of the world.

How it might have been: Bernini's original Italianate design for the Louvre east façade (top), versus the French classical colonnade that was eventually built

The King's French

The first edition of the *Académie française*'s dictionary appeared in 1694. Its pronouncements had an imperious Louis-Quatorzian ring to them. Only "fine usage" (*bel usage)*, as spoken in the presence of the monarch by gentlemen, orators, and poets, was recommended. Words deemed vulgar, regional, rustic, or plebeian were simply banned as unworthy of the King's French. In terms of pronunciation, the academy bore down on patois and dialect while devising rules for standardized spelling. Thanks to the academicians, for example, the French now eat *fromage* and *asperges* rather than *formage* and *asparges*. Many words regarded as old-fashioned or obsolete were barred, though the academicians retained many historic spellings (*corps, temps,* etc.) as well the mute *e* at the end of words. Altogether, they authorized complexities in the language that remain the bane of every schoolchild struggling with a *dictée.*

If the academies seemed unduly focused on patrolling the boundaries of good taste, they also served to support writers and intellectuals. Their commanding approach could have been stultifying. In practice, however, it proved to have a galvanizing effect, drawing the best minds of the era into the royal orbit. Most of the Grand Siècle's pantheon of literary greats—who included Corneille, Racine, Molière, La Fontaine, Charles Perrault, and Mme de Sévigné—owed some of their advancement to state patronage.

Louis also mobilized the best practitioners of the fine arts. In the early part of his reign, he worked closely with Colbert on architectural projects in the classical style that would make the Parisian capital a "new Rome," with triumphal arches to boot. But Louis rarely felt comfortable in the city, whose rambunctious culture was not to his taste. He began to spend more time and effort on transforming a former hunting lodge at rural Versailles into a palace worthy of Louis le Grand.

The Versailles project began in earnest in 1660, when Louis filched from Nicolas Fouquet three individuals who had been responsible for the construction and décor of the first minister's beautiful chateau at Vaux-le-Vicomte, some thirty miles southwest of Paris. The king gave the architect Louis Le Vau, the painter Charles Le Brun, and the garden designer André Le Nôtre free rein to reimagine Versailles as a wonder of the world. By 1682, they had transformed the site into a permanent exhibit of French art and architecture that attracted huge numbers of visitors from across the continent.

Versailles was a showcase, but it was a working showcase. Louis decided to relocate his ministers there. Members of the high aristocracy were also obliged to be present at court in person, as a way of weakening their provincial powerbases. Protocol was refined, complex, and strict, and extended from taste in fine art to table manners, relations between the sexes, fashionable dress, and much else besides. The royal court became a laboratory in which new rulings on *politesse* (politeness) and *civilité* (civility) by Louis and his royal academies could be tested in vivo.

The Sun of Versailles

The sun symbol was used as a motif throughout Versailles. The inscription reads, "Not unequal to many."

One of the most striking features of the Versailles showcase is the use of the solar motif throughout the palace. *Le roi soleil* ("the Sun King") had claimed the emblem as his own early in his reign. In 1653, at the age of fifteen, he danced in a court ballet as the sun god Apollo to reinforce the point. The decorative schema promoted at Versailles made Louis the solar center of his universe, the famous Hall of Mirrors reflecting his own glory back to him. Its ceiling was covered with paintings commemorating all the battles and famous moments in his reign, centered around the image of 1661: "Louis governs by himself."

There was little room in this universe for disagreement. Representative institutions within France were abolished under Louis XIV or were considerably weakened. Censorship remained fierce. Colbert slashed the number of printers in Paris and introduced a regulatory program that incentivized loyalty to the crown. He also worked closely with the *Lieutenant de Police* of Paris, a post created in 1667, whose incumbent enjoyed sweeping control over all aspects of city life, including the reporting of news and opinion.

Louis's crackdown on open expression ran into problems when it came to religion. Despite his claims to rule by divine right, his flamboyant reign was dogged by Jansenism, an austere spiritual tendency in Catholicism. In addition, he feared the Protestant community as a seedbed of dissenters and fifth columnists. Louis systematically chipped away the religious rights granted by his predecessors. With Counter-Reformation *dévots* cheering him on, the king mixed preaching and persuasion with campaigns of outright violence. From 1681, the royal government billeted dragoons (*dragons)* or mounted infantry in Protestant communities to enforce conversion to Catholicism. The *dragonnades* enraged Protestants throughout Europe and made Louis the object of international condemnation.

Finally, in 1685, Louis cut the Gordian knot and revoked Henry IV's Edict of Nantes. Protestantism was no longer tolerated in France. Apart from taking the shine off the monarchy's sunny reputation, the fallout had deeper repercussions as resentment grew. Many Protestants forced to convert to Catholicism continued to practice their faith clandestinely. Some openly rebelled. The so-called Camisard War in the Cévennes mountains (1702–1710) erupted as France was engaged in the War of the

Spanish Succession, forcing the king to drag much-needed troops away from the battlefront to pacify the region.

Other Protestants voted with their feet. Roughly two hundred thousand Huguenots left France, settling in the Dutch Republic, England, and Prussia, as well as other Protestant states in Germany. France's loss was its rivals' gain, with England and the Dutch Republic in particular benefiting from the immigration of skilled industrial workers. The Huguenot diaspora also fortified intellectual resistance to France across Protestant Europe. A loophole in Louis's censorship regime allowed the French-language *Gazette de Leyde*, as well as newspapers and pamphlets published in Amsterdam, Utrecht, The Hague, and elsewhere, to circulate unhindered throughout France by the royal mail.

In the final two decades of his reign, Louis found himself losing the propaganda battle. Compounding the injuries to the royal ego, his final campaigns in pursuit of European hegemony—notably the War of the League of Augsburg (1689–1697) and that of the Spanish Succession (1701–1714)–went badly. As warfare became globalized, its costs spiraled upward. Much of the Spanish conflict was fought in the Americas and in Mediterranean and Atlantic waters.

Vauban's Iron Belt

Between 1665 and 1707, the military engineer Vauban designed a series of magnificent fortresses guarding French ports and borders. This *ceinture de fer* was designed to stop invasion, especially of France's most recent territorial acquisitions. Making the nation's outer frontiers impenetrable to foreign enemies was also a good excuse to dismantle urban fortifications within, on the grounds they were now redundant. The iron belt thus helped make towns that had been so troublesome in the Wars of Religion and the Fronde less able to oppose the royal will.

France was creaking under the growing weight of warfare. Its agrarian economy was still weak and fragile, while its wealthiest inhabitants—the clergy, the nobility, and privileged city dwellers—bore little of the tax burden. Climate change only made things worse. The tendency of the Little Ice Age to spark extreme weather events culminated in devastating winters in 1693–1694 and 1709–1710 that produced the last big famines in French history. With disease and warfare also doing their bit, premature deaths may have exceeded two million over the period from 1689 to 1715, nearly a tenth of the population.

The last years of Louis XIV's long reign were undoubtedly the bleakest of the so-called *Grand Siècle*. On his deathbed in 1715, he admitted, "I have loved war too much." The era of the Sun King was in eclipse. Grim decades of war and privation had left the country in a dismal state, its military reputation much diminished, and its cultural grandeur heavily tarnished.

Champagne after the Funeral

Louis left a tough legacy for his successors. His heir, Louis XV, was a five-year-old child, so regency powers were enacted for the duke of Orléans, the new king's uncle. Orléans was the black sheep of the Bourbon family. He had been heartily despised by Louis XIV, and returned the compliment. Presenting himself as a new broom, he swiftly moved the royal court from Versailles back to Paris and began sweeping away the most authoritarian aspects of the old regime.

A Momentary Sparkle

Curiously, it was the English who invented champagne, notably through late seventeenth-century experiments with chemical methods for controlling fermentation and ways of producing robust bottles that could cope with sparkling wine. But it was France—in the person of the duke of Orléans—that made it the *vin du moment*. The glittering, hedonistic cultural atmosphere of the Regency, coming after Louis XIV's somber final years, made champagne's association with the new regime seem apt. Unfortunately for both Orléans and France, every bubble bursts.

Orléans's openness to novelty and innovation proved the undoing of the Regency. He embraced some of the wilder financial ideas of the Scottish-French economist John Law, who created a kind of Ponzi scheme based around fantasized profits to be derived from colonial investment in Louisiana. A huge financial bubble ensued, followed by an almighty crash that completely discredited Orléans and his efforts at reform.

The young Louis XV dispensed with any plans formulated under the Regency the moment he came of age. He could not return to Versailles quickly enough. Duly installed in 1722, he resurrected Louis XIV's political system in all its essentials. He also attempted to revive the reputation of his illustrious father, lauding the *Grand Siècle* of the Sun King and its civic and military triumphs—though not the ensuing state debts. Louis's XIV's

absolutism, religious intolerance, and impoverishment of his subjects were harder to paint over. In the last years of his reign, the
public had seen through the dazzling façade. Ominously for the
dynasty, public opinion would only grow stronger as the eighteenth
century progressed.

CHAPTER 4

FRANCE GOES GLOBAL

An Age of Revolutions (1720–1850)

France's 1789 Revolution was one of the defining moments of the modern age. Rising from the cultural and intellectual ferment of the Enlightenment, it provided a template for democratic change and a rich ideological matrix for future generations around the world to follow. Yet the material strength that France had built up abroad through global trade and colonial expansion was sapped by the almost endless Revolutionary and Napoleonic wars that ensued. France's presence outside Europe shrank drastically and had to be rebuilt from the ground up after 1815.

In the wake of the Revolution, France's course was marked by severe political turbulence. The country had no fewer than six regimes of wildly different character, passing from Bourbon absolutism to a constitutional monarchy (1789–1791), a republic (1792–1804), an empire (1804–1814), a restored Bourbon regime (1815–1830), and more liberal monarchy (1830–1838), before another revolution in 1848 briefly opened the door to a Second Republic and a return to some of the democratic ideas mapped out in the 1790s. But the enlightened notion of a French republic still divided opinion decades later and the eventual outcome was by no means certain.

France's Five Republics

In the years since the 1789 Revolution, France had not one but five republics, each with a different constitution:

First Republic (1792–1804)
Second Republic (1848–1852)
Third Republic (1870–1940)
Fourth Republic (1946–1958)
Fifth Republic (1958–the present)

Portrait of Voltaire from
the workshop of Nicolas de
Largillière (c. 1720)

Le Siècle des Lumières

The period after 1720 up to the 1789 Revolution was dominated by the intellectual and cultural movement known as the "Age of Light," or the Enlightenment. It was led by *philosophes*, natural philosophers and critical thinkers such as Voltaire, Montesquieu, Diderot, and Rousseau, who saw themselves as participants in a project to spread the light of reason for the benefit of all. Social progress was within reach for any society that conducted itself rationally and beneficently and that took advantage of advances in human knowledge and scientific endeavor.

The *philosophes* were highly critical of the Catholic Church. *Écrasez l'infâme!* ("Crush clerical infamy!") was Voltaire's motto. For him, as for others, the church, in conjunction with the absolutist state, acted as a brake on progress. Religious belief in scripture as the foundation of all knowledge was out of sync with Enlightenment trust in human reason. While church and state sought to dictate what people should think and feel, the *philosophes* preached freedom—the freedom of every individual to think, believe, know, write, debate, and act.

The *Encyclopédie,* the "Bible of the Enlightenment," the multi-authored, twenty-eight-volume work that Diderot and his friend d'Alembert co-edited between 1751 and 1772, was a compilation of human knowledge across all disciplinary domains, with no theological guardrails. It was subtitled "Dictionary of the Sciences, Arts, and Trades." Rather than reaching back to ancient Greece and Rome, the *Encyclopédie* looked beyond Europe to the new world of knowledge opened up by the expansion of empire and global commerce. Articles provided copious information on the world's flora, fauna, and mineral resources.

Diderot dipped down within society too, drawing up information, ideas, and practices from social strata below the elite, particularly where these related to social utility. There was, Diderot proclaimed, "more intelligence, wisdom, and consequence in a stocking-making machine" than in any "system of metaphysics." By learning from all domains of human endeavor, even the humblest, Diderot expressed the hope "that we may thereby become virtuous and happy and that we may not die without having deserved well of humankind."

Diderot's Enlightenment Mission

This shall be our motto. No quarter for the superstitious, the ignorant, or for fools, malefactors, or tyrants. I would see our brothers united in zeal for truth, goodness, and beauty. It is not enough for us to know more than Christians; we must show that we are better and that science has done more for humankind than divine grace.

Diderot to Voltaire, 1762

One of the biggest hurdles for this band of brothers was censorship. In the course of their careers, a great many Enlightenment luminaries suffered government wrath in the form of imprisonment. For the *Encyclopédie* project to stay afloat, contributors had to make any potentially subversive points obliquely, sensitively, and with sundry nods and winks, trusting that the official censor would pass lightly over them. The ruse worked. Publication of the project in full was a triumph of optimism, vision, entrepreneurial stamina, and editorial cunning.

The success of the *Encyclopédie* signaled the inability of the Bourbon state to prevent the circulation of new ideas. In fact, no European state was capable of quelling the relentless rise of print or of audiences for the printed word. The eighteenth century saw the rapid growth of the reading public. Twice as many people were literate by the end of the period than at the beginning. Moreover, busy printing presses delivered a more secular, "enlightened" reading diet than in the past, when religious titles had dominated. Popular tastes now ranged from *belles-lettres*, drama, poetry, and opera through to law, history, political economy, travel writing, popular science, agronomy, gardening, fashion, and fiction.

A Worldwide Web of Letters

The novel was in many ways the Enlightenment's breakthrough genre. A great favorite was the epistolary novel, in which the plot was narrated through the exchange of letters. The eighteenth century was a golden age of letter-writing, with multiple networks of individuals linked across countries and continents. Epistolary novels offered a glimpse of this private world—and delivered the first genuine bestsellers of the modern age. Readers lined up around the block to secure a copy of Rousseau's tear-jerking *Julie,*

Remade by Hollywood as *Dangerous Liaisons* in 1988, Laclos's erotic thriller
Les Liaisons dangereuses continues to thrill readers and viewers alike.

ou la Nouvelle Héloise (1761), while Laclos's chillingly erotic *Les Liaisons dangereuses* (1782) was an underground hit.

Public literacy was reinforced by a large and dynamic newspaper press. Political news still needed to be handled with care, though an unfiltered supply of news and opinion trickled in from the francophone press abroad. A deluge of inventive new titles also made Richelieu's government-endorsed *Gazette* seem stuffy and archaic. Most newspapers carried international, social, and cultural news, while there were specialized periodicals too for the professional sector and lovers of fashion and quizzes. The press formed an interwoven chain of enlightened opinion, "a kind of confraternity, spread out throughout the kingdom," as one editor rather grandiloquently put it.

The most illustrious *philosophes*, the influencers of their day, used this worldwide web of readers and writers to extol their own talents, diffuse their views, and help to construct *l'opinion publique.*

Popularized by Rousseau's novel *Julie*, the term enshrined an idea of society as a collection of individuals keen to exchange ideas and operate at the same level, rather than via some legal hierarchy of orders and corporate bodies. Seen in this way, public opinion was a kind of democratic tribunal, composed of citizens who passed their collective judgment on matters of public interest.

It was a somewhat idealistic view. As with new media in any age, the print boom included scandal sheets, pornography, celebrity gossip, and fashion crazes among the more high-minded news and Enlightenment views. Even so, this positive, democratic notion of public opinion became a force in the land.

> *Public opinion*: an invisible power that without treasury or armed force lays down its laws to city, court, and palaces.
> Royal minister Jacques Necker, 1781

Paris and the Art of Living

Nowhere was the new force of public opinion more evident than in the French capital. "Paris," declared the writer Marivaux, "is the world. The rest of the earth is nothing but its suburbs." The city welcomed an effervescent flood of writers, intellectuals, artists, tourists, and outsiders of every description who flocked to enjoy the city's many pleasures—carnal, it must be admitted, as well as cultural. Learned societies, salons, coffee houses, opera houses, concert halls, reading rooms, libraries, public gardens, promenades, and masonic lodges acted as poles for urban sociability for an ever more vocal elite. If Versailles retained some of its cachet with the upwardly mobile royalty of Europe, it was the capital rather than the royal court that claimed the heart of an "enlightened" French public. Paris put the Sun King's palace in the shade.

Parisians extolled their city as the world capital of the arts, sciences, and modes of civilized living. It was the heart, too, of an increasingly French-speaking world. French had become the language of international diplomacy and the *lingua franca* of a cosmopolitan European elite. Rulers such as Catherine the Great of Russia and Prussia's Frederick the Great communicated in the language. "If something isn't clear," declared the author Rivarol, "then it isn't French"—a totally fallacious claim but one with remarkable influence on practitioners of science, technology, the arts, and natural philosophy, all of whom prized clarity of expression. And if *clarté* made French the language of academies and salons, the seductive charm of *galanterie* made it the language of the bedroom too. Casanova, a Venetian, thought, wrote, and made love in French.

For all its transnational success, French was still not the first language of most French people. In France as across Europe, speaking, reading, and writing in the French language gave elites a sense of commonality as well as distance from the lower social orders, among whom patois, dialect, and other languages entirely still reigned supreme. Despite its democratic potential, an Enlightenment education was largely confined to the French-speaking middle and upper classes rather than the general public.

The World in a Cup

Consumer goods were another matter. Voltaire once imagined a Parisian chambermaid starting her day wearing a light cotton dress (from India), drinking tea (from China) or coffee (from Turkey) sweetened with sugar (from the Caribbean) out of a porcelain cup (from Japan), before going on to take snuff (from Louisiana). Even though Voltaire deplored the fact, a Parisian style of living required global sources.

This light French breakfast was made possible by the rapid globalization of trade since the final doldrum years of Louis XIV's reign, as well as by the recovery of the economy. The population grew by 40 percent, stimulated by a rise in living standards and an end to the devastating waves of plague that had swept France for centuries—the last big outbreak, in Marseille in 1720, was confined to the south. Communications marked an important change. A modernized road system enabled the secure and speedy transmission of people and goods alongside the letters and newspapers carried by the state postal service. Mid-century, it took up to two weeks for a package from Paris to reach Marseille. By 1789, the delivery time was down to four days.

The Canal du Midi

French waterways were equally busy in this period. Constructed in 1681, the Canal du Midi came into its own in the eighteenth century. It linked with existing river trading networks, effectively joining the Atlantic coast to the Mediterranean. The resulting *Canal des Deux Mers* was a tremendous stimulus to the whole economy of the southwest, opening it up to world trade.

These economic changes had a marked effect on everyday living. Spending rose on every aspect of material comfort, from diet and domestic furnishings to reading matter, while new trade networks put everything from New World tobacco to Indian cotton within reach of those from relatively humble backgrounds, including Voltaire's chambermaid.

Sugar from the Caribbean was the Enlightenment's addictive drug of choice, and its impact on the popular diet meant that chronic toothache was a painful sign of the times. Combined with coffee, increasingly sourced from the Caribbean rather than the Ottoman empire, it also transformed drinking habits. Imports of eastern porcelain targeted high-end consumers, but experimentation by French ceramicists soon put cheap china at the disposal of the popular classes. Lighter textiles, inspired by Indian printed cottons, passed into general usage too.

Enlightenment Paris became a consumerist showcase for luxury products. Mercantilist businesses established by Colbert—to which Louis XV added the Sèvres porcelain works in 1756—helped to feed an endless fashion cycle for high-end consumer goods. Fine furniture-making and glass-finishing work in the Faubourg Saint-Antoine and jewelry around the Place Dauphine on the Ile de la Cité prospered as never before. The duke of Orléans allowed his Parisian residence, the Palais-Royal, to be used as a prototype shopping mall. The adjoining Rue Saint-Honoré became the dynamo of internationally admired and much imitated Paris fashion.

The Rue Saint-Honoré fashion doll

Female fashion designers (*marchandes de mode*) on Paris's Rue Saint-Honoré viewed themselves as the avant-garde of women's wear. They waxed and buffed this reputation by producing fashion dolls on an almost industrial scale. Roughly a foot tall and dressed in the latest height of fashion, these *poupées à la mode* or *poupées de la Rue Saint-Honoré* were shipped out to dressmakers and potential buyers throughout Europe and North America throughout the century. Marie-Antoinette nurtured her famous taste for fashion from caseloads of the mannequins received as a teenager in the Viennese court. Even when France and England were at war, *poupées à la mode* were given special diplomatic passes to cross the Channel.

Ports on the Atlantic seaboard prospered in this period, many such as Bordeaux, La Rochelle, Nantes, and Saint-Malo by specializing in the slave trade. France had turned its hand to the trade in earnest following its humiliation by Britain in the global struggles of the Seven Years' War (1756–1763). Defeat at the hands of "Perfidious Albion" (Treacherous England) meant the loss of Canada and part of Louisiana as well as territory in western Africa, while the French presence in India was reduced to just five coastal trading posts. Louis XV's minister Choiseul masterminded a complete reset of French foreign policy. Thoughts of colonial settlement and territorial expansion on the North American model were put to one side. Instead,

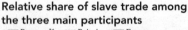

Relative share of slave trade among the three main participants

Portugal* Britain France

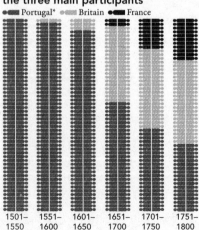

1501–1550 1551–1600 1601–1650 1651–1700 1701–1750 1751–1800

France focused its attention on plantation colonies that relied on imports of African slaves.

France was a relative latecomer to a trade initially dominated by the Spanish and Portuguese, into which the English and the Dutch were also making inroads. It soon made up for lost time. Maybe forty thousand African slaves were shipped to French colonies during the entire seventeenth century. This number rose to nearly four hundred thousand in the first half of the eighteenth. A further 750,000 enslaved people would be transported before 1800, bringing France closer to the vast numbers trafficked by the British and Portuguese.

The Bitter Fruit of Sugar Island

The island of Saint-Domingue was the jewel in France's colonial crown. There were other Caribbean islands with slave plantations—notably Guadeloupe and Martinique—while slaves were also used in the Mascarene island colonies (notably Réunion and Mauritius) in the Indian Ocean. But Saint-Domingue's production was on a vastly different scale. It was the world's "Sugar Island" and the hub of by far the most dynamic sector of French trade. Profits fed a substantial slave-owning elite in the islands, who participated eagerly in the sinister side of the Atlantic world's sweet-toothed, cosmopolitan culture.

Paris, capital of the Enlightenment and beacon of human progress, largely turned a blind eye to the slave trade and blithely enjoyed the profits it generated. The city was a major conduit for investment in the trade, as well as an eager client. Enslaved African infants dressed as decorative lackeys became a cherished accessory in the homes of the wealthy. In 1770, the *Histoire des Deux-Indes* by the Abbé Raynal, assisted by Diderot, offered an excoriating critique of the cruelty involved in slavery, though little was said about the destruction of African communities involved.

It was only in the late 1780s that a French anti-slavery movement emerged on the back of British abolitionism. By then, the rapid buildup in slave numbers, the violence in labor relations on plantations, and signs of resistance were stirring unease among the colonial elite, who muttered warningly of a "Black Spartacus" emerging to lead a huge anti-French slave revolt. With all eyes turned to the Caribbean, metropolitan France erupted in revolution.

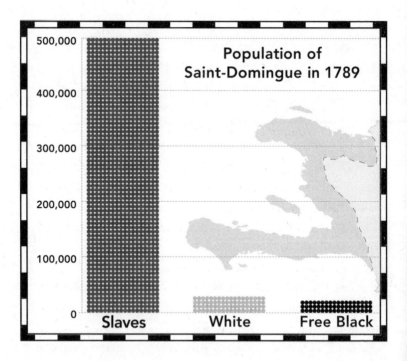

A Revolutionary Decade

May 1789	Estates General
June 1789	Estates General becomes National Constituent Assembly
1789–1792	**Constitutional Monarchy**
September 1791	Constitution ratified
October 1791	New Legislative Assembly
April 1792	War on European powers begins
August 1792	Overthrow of King Louis XVI
1792–1804	**The First Republic**
September 1792	New National Convention meets, Republic declared
Mid 1793–mid 1794	The Terror
July 1793	New constitution (never implemented)
July 1794	Fall of Robespierre, beginning of the move to the political right
1795	New constitution
1795	Regime of the Directory
November 1799	Bonaparte coup d'état The Consulate established
1804	End of First Republic Declaration of **Napoleonic Empire**

The Seeds of Revolution

Conservatives would later argue that the 1789 Revolution had been caused by the Enlightenment. It was, they said, "all the fault of Voltaire and Rousseau." The *philosophes* and their allies had eroded respect for the established order.

Undeniably, the Enlightenment hugely influenced the course and content of the Revolution. But a cause? The *philosophes* hardly offered a preordained script for revolution. Indeed, their views on ways of effecting political change varied greatly. Voltaire, for example, envisioned an enlightened monarch pushing through reforms at the expense of vested interests, while Montesquieu favored the English model of mixed monarchy. Rousseau showed a more democratic vision in his *Social Contract* (1762), though this was based on the small republics of classical antiquity, where citizens could gather face-to-face within the agora to make decisions. This kind of direct democracy seemed impossible to imagine in France, the largest state in Europe, where the population was approaching twenty-eight million.

The seeds of 1789 were largely sown by the global politics of the era. The financial cost of Louis XIV's wars was a millstone around the neck of government throughout the century. In addition, the rocketing costs of the Seven Years' War were grim even for the victor, Britain, whose efforts to reset its own finances provoked the revolt of its American colonists. Louis XVI could not resist the opportunity to exact revenge on the British by entering the American War of Independence (1776–1783) on the colonists' side. Victory was a pyrrhic one for France. Serially imprudent financial and international policies gave the monarchy a debt mountain to deal with in the aftermath.

The French Revolution was more the fruit of impending state bankruptcy than of enlightened thinking. But the Enlightenment certainly shaped its growth. With no easy solution to the financial crisis on the horizon, the government tried something new: consultation with public opinion. In 1788, in a move completely absent from the absolutist playbook, Louis summoned the Estates General to meet the following year. This national consultative body had last met in 1614. Its task now was to see if tough financial reforms could be pushed through by eliciting popular consent.

It was a risky wager, and it rebounded catastrophically. The supreme tribunal of public opinion proved to be singularly unimpressed by the monarchy's plans. Once the Estates General met, the government found itself outwitted by the deputies of the Third Estate, whom Louis instructed to meet separately from the other two orders, the clergy and the nobility. The commoners ignored the royal command and obstinately refused to play ball with the king over a bailout unless the crown consented to constitutional reform.

What is the Third Estate?

1. *What is the Third Estate? Everything.*
2. *What has it been hitherto in the political order? Nothing.*
3. *What does it desire to be? To become something.*

> Abbé Emmanuel-Joseph Siéyès,
> *Qu'est -ce que le Tiers État?* (1789)

Siéyès's widely read pamphlet promoted the view that the Third Estate of commoners was more productive and useful to society than the two "privileged orders" of clergy and nobility put together.

The intransigence of the Third Estate went down well with the general public. Louis was forced to agree to the Estates General's becoming a National Assembly that would devise a new constitution. When the king appeared to be backing down from his promises, Parisians stormed the notorious Bastille prison on July 14,

1789, obliging him to accept the inevitable. Sovereignty was now in the hands of the elected representatives of the French nation. A new national emblem, the *tricolore*, which conjoined the red and blue ceremonial colors of the city of Paris with the white of the Bourbon monarchy, was invented at this moment of apparent national union.

The Taking of the Bastille by the painter Jean-Pierre Houël, who witnessed the Revolution and its aftermath

Deputies also exploited the crisis caused by bad harvests in 1787 and 1788, which had generated widespread hunger and discontent in towns and the countryside alike. When in the late summer of 1789 the peasantry took to arms to prevent a reversal of their gains, the assembly decreed the abolition of feudalism, followed by the nationalization—and subsequent sale—of land belonging to the church. These moves attached much of the peasantry to the political chariot of the revolution.

Tasked to provide France with a written constitution, the national assembly set about wiping away the alleged vices of what they called the former regime (*l'Ancien Régime*) and starting with a clean slate. On August 26, 1789, the famous Declaration of the Rights of Man set out the general maxims for a universalist constitution. Its stirring opening lines—*Les hommes naissent et demeurent libres et égaux en droits*—were lifted almost wholesale from Rousseau's *Social Contract*. Starting from the principle that sovereignty should no longer be embodied in the ruler but in the nation, the document declared that any political system should be grounded in individual freedoms of expression, religious belief, and economic activity, guaranteed by the law.

A Birthright for All Ages

"Man is born free and everywhere he is in chains."
Jean-Jacques Rousseau, *The Social Contract*, 1762

"Men are born and remain free and equal in rights."
                    Declaration of the Rights of Man, 1789

"All human beings are born free and equal in dignity and rights."
                    Universal Declaration of Human Rights,
                                    United Nations, 1948

The lineage of the Declaration of the Rights of Man marks it out as the birth certificate of the modern age, even though it postdates the Declaration of Independence by more than a decade.

The Declaration of the Rights of Man set the agenda for democratic debate and conflict throughout the 1790s. The key question seemed to be how its universalist rhetoric squared with the pragmatics of power and the scale of resources to hand. Seating arrangements in the assembly hall created the notion of a "Left" and a "Right" that was to endure in democratic politics worldwide. But there were many shades of opinion on both sides. For example, the draft constitution proposed representative democracy and a property franchise. Did this mean only those with a certain amount of wealth could enjoy all the rights? Did the "rights of man" include slaves? Or women? The feminist and abolitionist Olympe de Gouges produced a "Declaration of the Rights of Women" in 1791 aimed at persuading people that it should. But her argument went unheeded. The National Constituent Assembly valued individual freedom over equality and preferred liberal rather than radical answers to such questions.

The assembly's work was formidable. There was hardly a corner of public life and institutions—administrative, judicial, religious, cultural, social, and economic, as well as political—where its new, rationalizing broom was not in evidence. It was particularly sweeping in matters of religion. Root-and-branch reorganization of the Catholic Church, in a reform known as the Civil Constitution of the Clergy, upset the papacy as well as many French Catholics, creating a significant and long-lasting line of political division.

Last Days of the Ancien Régime

Although most of France seemed enthused by 1789, Louis XVI was certainly not. While paying lip-service to the new arrangements, he sought covertly to protect the nobility and its privileges, to return the church to traditional forms, and to restore his own sovereignty—and dignity. Many nobles took refuge abroad. The newly arrived *émigrés* of London and Vienna put pressure on European rulers to intervene militarily in France, pointing to the rash of revolutionary associations now mushrooming across Europe. Free thinkers the world over had welcomed 1789 as inaugurating an era of national self-determination and global peace. But now an international crisis loomed.

The Paris Jacobin Club

The Paris Jacobin Club (named after the former monastery where it met) was the most influential political association of its day. In the brief period of its existence from 1789 to 1794, the society brought together deputies from the national assembly with politically minded and well-heeled members of the general public. Its debates helped set the tone of the assembly itself. From an early stage, affiliations from provincial clubs were encouraged. By 1793–1794, these probably numbered in excess of five thousand, with as many as half a million individual members. The Paris club became increasingly aligned with its most high-profile and divisive member, Maximilien Robespierre. The reactionary elite of Europe and America used "Jacobin" as a vituperative term of abuse for a century or more.

In April 1792, revolutionary France went to war against Austria and Prussia. Almost at once, the king recoiled from the cause. With the war going spectacularly badly and allied forces bearing down on Paris, fears of royal treachery stimulated an uprising in the city. On August 10, 1792, the monarchy was overthrown. New elections were called, with universal suffrage—at least for men—for the first time in world history. The first act of the new assembly, the National Convention, was to proclaim a republic on September 21.

King Louis XVI was tried by the assembly and guillotined on January 21 the following year. The execution was the trigger for Britain and other remaining European powers to ally militarily against the new republic. With sea and land wars going equally badly, the new regime was in danger of being stillborn.

Madame la Guillotine

The French revolutionaries regarded the guillotine as a humane invention, as it replaced the horrific death-by-torture of burning, hanging, quartering, or drowning administered to criminals under the former penal code. Prior to 1789, only the privileged elite lost their heads. Charles I of England had been decapitated in 1649 by axe, for example, while French noblemen sentenced to death

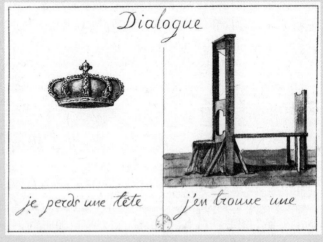

Crown: "I lose a head"; guillotine: "I find one" (1793)

were decapitated by sword, a difficult task calling for a steady hand. The swift, mechanical dispatch offered by the guillotine was therefore a back-handed nod to the victim's dignity as a citizen. Louis XVI was among some 2,600 souls guillotined in Paris from 1792 to 1795. *Madame la Guillotine* or *La Veuve* ("The Widow") was employed by the French state until 1977.

The Terror

In the event, the republic survived the crisis years of 1792–1794. The immediate military threat was repelled by heroic French resistance at Verdun, followed by a resounding victory over the Prussians at Valmy, which stopped the advance for the time being. The conflict had not gone away, however. The national assembly put the country on a more permanent war footing.

Individual freedoms were drastically curtailed. Authoritarian power was placed in the hands of a war council, the Committee of Public Safety, drawn from deputies within the Convention, who had to face up to internal turbulence as well as military maneuvers on the front. Roused by hostility to church reform, the area around the Vendée department in western France erupted in open civil war. Many other areas remained restive about the direction that the Revolution was taking.

This period is often called the Terror because of the government's naked use of coercion, intimidation, and violence, as symbolized by the work of the Revolutionary Tribunal and its instrument of choice, the guillotine. Terror found its most vocal ideologist in Maximilien Robespierre. A former provincial lawyer, he became a leader of the radical left-wing Montagnard faction and was a dominant figure in the Paris Jacobin Club, which gave him a national profile. Robespierre and the Jacobins also mobilized Parisian street radicals known as *sans-culottes*.

Sans-culottes en armes: character portraits by Jean-Baptiste Lesueur

Sans-culottes

Parisian militants drawn from the middle and lower classes of the city were nicknamed *sans-culottes* for ostentatiously preferring workmen's trousers to the knee breeches (*culottes*) associated with *Ancien Régime* gentility. The sans-culottes were one of the main driving forces behind the radicalization of the Revolution in 1792–1794.

Robespierre and his allies headed a power bloc comprising the Jacobin network, the Montagnards, and the sans-culottes that aimed to crush any opposition. Policies were introduced to muster the bulk of the population across the country behind the Revolution and the war. The Montagnards first cleared the decks by brutally removing their rivals, known as Brissotins or Girondins. This allowed them to introduce a raft of sweeping social policies: the radical democratic constitution of 1793 (held in reserve until the end of the war), land reforms favoring the peasantry, price controls on basic commodities, and wide-ranging social welfare measures. A Revolutionary Calendar was created marking the epochal moment that a republic was declared.

Revolutionary Times

In 1793, the Julio-Gregorian calendar was replaced by a new Revolutionary Calendar dating from September 21, 1792. There were still twelve calendar months but the seven-day week was replaced by a ten-day *décade*. Never truly popular, the calendar was wound down under Napoleon. Other acts of reforming zeal during the Terror, such as turning churches into "Temples of Reason"—Notre-Dame cathedral included—fared little better. Plans to replace the chaotic mess of traditional weights and measures with a metric system had a happier outcome.

M.M.J. ROBERSPIERRE

Engraving after a portrait by Guérin, 1789

This radical shot in the arm gave ordinary French people something to fight for and turned the European conflict into a patriotic war. Galvanized by the turn in the Revolution, a new enthusiasm for radical politics found expression in a plethora of political clubs, which, along with newspapers and pamphlets, played a crucial recruiting role. Mass conscription—the so-called *levée en masse*—swelled the ranks of the army to meet the military challenge. What raw recruits lacked in firearms training and military discipline they made up for in revolutionary fervor. Before long, the republic's sprawling makeshift forces started to gain victories over the battle-hardened standing armies of the European powers.

By the middle of 1794, all foreign armies had been driven off French territory. At this point, the Montagnards split over the best way forward. While Robespierre favored ramping up the Terror and introducing even more radical social policies for religion, welfare, and education, others had had enough: military success should allow a slackening of the state of emergency and a return to constitutional normalcy. A buildup of tension was followed by a day of action on July 27, 1794 in which Robespierre was overthrown and his faction guillotined.

Despite the ferocious reputation it acquired, the Terror does not weigh excessively on the scales of history in terms of its body count. Some 2,600 individuals were guillotined in Paris, while over 250,000 died in France as a whole, mainly in civil war zones and particularly around the Vendée. This represented around 1 percent of the population, a similar percentage to lives lost in the American War of Independence, which, like the French Revolution, was very much a civil war. Revolutionary and Napoleonic wars ending in 1815 would cause the deaths of well over a million Frenchmen and certainly more of France's enemies. The European slave trade would claim many, many more lives over the century.

Revolution and Decolonization

The Caribbean offers a point of comparison. In 1791, a slave revolt broke out in Saint-Domingue. The island was soon in the grip of civil war, with atrocities on both sides. The rebels were led by the charismatic and resourceful ex-slave Toussaint L'Ouverture, and their ideas were a heady mix of African and American ideology, with a dash of French Rights-of-Man rhetoric for good measure.

The National Convention formally abolished slavery on February 4, 1794. In fact, they were beaten to it by their commissioner, Léger-Félicité Sonthonax, who had issued an emancipation decree the previous year, driven less by ideological concerns than the hope this might encourage the enslaved population of the French islands to fight the British.

In the event, the "Black Jacobin" and his followers refused to accept either concession or to desist from calls for independence. L'Ouverture was eventually captured by the French in 1802 and deported to France, where he would die in jail. But this did not prevent Saint-Domingue from winning its liberation struggle and declaring its independence as Haiti in 1804. Civil war had left a third of the population dead, mostly slaves: 180,000 out of a prior population of around 550,000. Despite this death toll, the Haitian Revolution was in many ways as much a world-historic event as 1789. The first successful slave revolt of modern times was also the first war of decolonization by non-whites.

The Political Legacy of Terror

Numbers aside, the Terror had a disproportionate and divisive impact on the shape of French politics for the next century or more. The main political currents within France would come to be defined by their relationship to the Terror. The political left came to look on it as a patriotic moment when Jacobin centralized power saved France from rapacious European neighbors, promoted egalitarian welfare policies, and built democratic institutions. Political centrists, a more ill-defined group that prioritized individual freedoms, accepted the liberal principles of 1789 but rejected the Terror as an unfortunate and avoidable deviation from the Revolution's core values.

By contrast, the political right saw the Revolution itself as the problem, with the Terror an inevitable and atrocious consequence of 1789. The right, grounded in strong Catholic support, continued to back the "legitimist" cause of the Bourbon monarchy. Following the death in prison of Louis XVI's infant son, his brother became pretender to the crown. Holed up in exile, the future Louis XVIII rejected the Revolution and all its works.

This divided setup was to receive one further fracture with the emergence in 1799 of the Revolution's greatest general, Napoleon Bonaparte. His seizure of power in a coup d'état brought a fourth element into an existing political landscape composed of legitimist right, Jacobin left, and liberal center—namely, Bonapartism.

Discord and Division

The 1790s were a decade of violent and volatile politics. In 1794, deputies of all political complexions cooperated in Robespierre's demise, but they saw eye to eye on precious little else. Right-wing deputies initially set the pace, suppressing the Parisian sans-culottes movement when it took to the barricades, then closing down the Jacobin Club. They compelled the National Convention to retreat from the radical welfare policies of the Terror, proposing instead a reversion to free-market economics—which caused something close to famine in the terrible winter of 1794–1795. A more tolerant attitude toward the church replaced sans-culottes "dechristianization." A new constitution in 1795 brought back a property franchise and replaced the radicalism of the Jacobin Constitution of 1793 with something like the liberal values of 1789–1791.

The new, post-1795 regime, the Directory, proved unable to stabilize the ship. Deeply etched memories of terror caused frictions that were aggravated by the growth of monarchist sentiment in the country. Coups and countercoups punctuated the political drama. Warfare made matters worse. What began in 1792 as a war of national defense had snowballed into a war of expansion. When it went well, plunder and the incorporation of new territories into France helped the conflict pay for itself. When it went badly, there was a financial shortfall, a political crisis, and a lurch to either the political left or right.

"A New Caesar"

The regime's reliance on a state of perpetual war forced it to give successful generals their head. Of these, Bonaparte was by far the most spectacular. Appointed commander on the unpromising Italian front in 1796, the young Bonaparte not only won many battles but soon brought the whole Italian peninsula under French control, changing the shape of the war. Sister Republics—essentially pro-French satellite regimes—were established throughout the Italian peninsula and in other areas of French domination.

> On May 15, 1796, General Bonaparte entered Milan at the head of that young army which had lately crossed the Lodi bridge and taught the world that after so many centuries Caesar and Alexander had a successor.
>
> Stendhal, *The Charterhouse of Parma*, 1839

The politicians in Paris thought they could deal with Bonaparte's growing authority and charisma by packing him off on an expedition to Egypt in 1798, to establish a French base from which to threaten British power in India. Yet a further crisis at home caused by a downturn in the war in Europe led to his return and seizure of power. He established the Consulate, with himself as First Consul and very much in the driver's seat. In 1804 he would upgrade himself to Emperor, ending the First Republic.

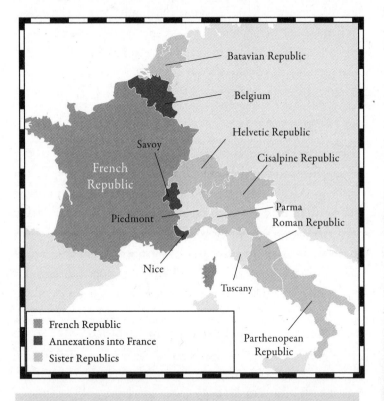

Batavian Republic

Belgium

Helvetic Republic

Savoy

Cisalpine Republic

French Republic

Parma

Piedmont

Roman Republic

Nice

Tuscany

Parthenopean Republic

- ◼ French Republic
- ◼ Annexations into France
- ◼ Sister Republics

Napoleon in Egypt

The military and strategic aspects of Bonaparte's Egyptian campaign were complemented by a scientific expedition involving over 150 scientists and scholars—men of letters, artists, geologists, chemists, engineers, and others.

Their aim was to discover more about the land, history, natural history, culture, and language of the area. The mission managed to discover the Rosetta stone and is credited, along with the widespread looting of numerous

sites and artifacts, with the birth of Orientalism. Bonaparte himself used the expedition for personal propaganda: he posed as an enlightened patron of the arts and sciences and as the liberator of the Egyptian people from their Muslim oppressors. His claims went down better in Paris than in Cairo.

Napoleon in Egypt, as imagined several decades later by the French Orientalist painter Jean-Léon Gérôme

Napoleon set about ending the internal discord of the 1790s on his own terms. He retained a written constitution, but quietly deleted the Rights of Man. He cultivated an ostentatious court on *Ancien Régime* lines, and ruled by imperial decree. He relied heavily on a strong, centralized bureaucracy and appointed loyal prefects to the departments into which France was now divided, powerful successors to the pre-1789 provincial Intendants. Heedless of individual freedoms, he came down heavily on the expression of political dissent. The number of newspapers fell precipitously. Those that remained in business shoveled out Napoleonic propaganda.

"The Revolution is over," Napoleon proclaimed on one occasion, and one can see what he meant. Yet on another occasion he declared, "I am the Revolution." For he also embodied much about the values and gains of 1789. He viewed social mobility, as guaranteed by equality before the law, as a key Revolutionary legacy in which he was personally invested. It was unimaginable that a young petty noble of Corsican provenance in his twenties could have been promoted to the military high command before 1789.

Napoleon continued educational and legal reforms begun in the 1790s. The 1804 civil code (the *Code Napoleon*) became a beacon of the legal system, despite its socially conservative and sexist bias. An 1801 Concordat with Rome settled the religious discord that had marred the 1790s and, by getting the papacy to endorse his regime, won Napoleon the undying gratitude of the Catholic peasantry. While recognizing Catholicism as the faith of the majority of the French people, he kept the church at arm's length from the education system. Establishing freedom of belief, he also subsidized the Jewish and Protestant communities.

Despite posing as a peacemaker and presiding over a general peace in 1802–1803, war was Napoleon's métier. His legendary victories over European enemies allowed him to build up a huge continental empire. At its base was a much-expanded France that extended outward into northern Spain, Italy, northern Germany, and the Low Countries. This was encased within a circle of puppet regimes and vassal states, in charge of which Napoleon placed members of his extended family. Napoleon also brought the other

Continental great powers (notably Austria and Prussia) into the French orbit. Bloated by Napoleonic expansion, France bore comparison in terms of size with the very different empire of Charlemagne.

The downside of this focus on Europe was the loss of an overseas empire. The blockade on French ports enforced by Britain's Royal Navy from 1793 to 1815 severed ties between France and its colonies, which tumbled one by one into British hands. Napoleon had not totally given up on further expansion, as was evident from his secret decision in 1801 to purchase the vast territory of Louisiana in North America from Spain. Yet in 1803 he changed his mind, selling it to the United States in the so-called Louisiana Purchase. Similarly, in 1802, he tried to reintroduce slavery to France's remaining West Indian islands, including civil war torn Saint-Domingue. In the event, his forces failed to deliver and Haitian independence was declared, while Martinique and Guadeloupe fell into British hands until 1815.

Napoleon's continental empire compensated for 'his global losses. Indeed, France treated its European territories in a highly colonial manner. In the early 1790s, the revolutionaries had envisioned bringing aid to peoples across Europe struggling for their freedom. Belgian, Dutch, German, Swiss, and Italian self-proclaimed Jacobins had welcomed French armies with open arms. But they soon discovered that their liberators felt no compunction about becoming their rulers. Any thoughts of self-determination, independence or democracy were soon quashed, while new taxes and onerous recruitment policies for France's ever-expanding armies constituted a heavy levy.

It was a mixed legacy. France brought its laws to conquered territories, plus constitutional government, the abolition of feudalism, the nationalization and sale of church lands, its civil code, equality before the law, and religious freedom. Yet these "enlightened" policies proved divisive when imposed from above. The use of plunder was extended to the looting of great artworks, which Napoleon brought ostentatiously to Paris.

Napoleon the Collector

The plundering of artworks did not start with Napoleon, but he was exceptionally good at it, happily looting wherever his campaigning took him across Europe and into Egypt. In 1798, he celebrated his haul in a huge procession in Paris that featured the bronze horses from St. Mark's Square in Venice, the Venus de Milo, the Apollo Belvedere, the Laocoön sculpture, and crateloads of Raphaels, Correggios, rare manuscripts, and more. This display of the spoils of conquest was justified by the notion that repatriating the work to Paris would allow them to flourish and educate humanity from the heartlands of the French republic. Many of these works ended up in the Louvre, by now an art museum rather than a royal palace. Despite a measure of restitution in 1815, many are still there.

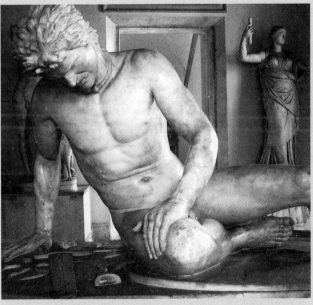

The Dying Gaul, one of many ancient artworks taken by Napoleon from Rome and one of the few returned

The Napoleonic empire was proudly and programmatically Francocentric. Military commanders, prefects, and Bonaparte family members all reported directly to Paris and prioritized French interests in directing government business. Economic strategy was grounded in Napoleon's maxim, "France before everything." Consequently, manufacturing outside France that undermined French producers was deliberately hobbled, while terms of trade were set to ensure that the French had first pickings of raw materials for their own industries. The Empire aimed to produce prosperity within France—at the expense of Europe, if necessary.

The Napoleonic Empire largely delivered on its promises of wealth for France, until harvest-driven crises from 1809 onward spoiled the picture. As ever, the British did their best to aggravate matters. Britain inveigled its own manufactured goods onto the continent, puncturing Napoleon's protectionist bubble. And from 1808 the British army established itself on the Iberian peninsula, joining with local politicians and guerrilla forces to resist French rule.

To Napoleon's "Spanish ulcer" was added Russian frostbite. The failure of the Emperor's armed invasion to bring the Russian czar to heel in 1812 cost France an army, which was destroyed in the disastrous winter retreat from Moscow. Napoleon's popularity in France sagged disastrously, while Italians and Germans as well as Spaniards rose up against their French oppressors. In 1815, Napoleon lost the Battle of Waterloo. He spent his last years marooned in the South Atlantic on Saint Helena, an outpost of British imperialism, which had proved more resilient than France's continental and overseas empires.

The Providential Leader

Napoleon had gone for good, but he had brought charisma and populism to French politics. His rise from relative obscurity had also hardwired into French political culture the notion of a providential leader who would pull the country out of the doldrums and lead it roughshod to glory. Napoleon III, Clemenceau, and Charles de Gaulle are notable examples of politicians who sought to tap into this myth, following Napoleon's lead in nurturing a cult of personality through a docile press.

Napoleon Crossing the Alps, mythologized by the painter
Jacques-Louis David

Napoleon's other great legacy was a new and tumultuous phase in the Age of Revolutions. The emperor's decision in 1808 to place his brother Joseph on the Spanish throne triggered a chain of unrest across the Atlantic world, which led in time to most Spanish and Portuguese colonies, achieving independence. The year 1820 saw revolutionary uprisings in Spain, Portugal, Italy, and Greece, though these proved largely unsuccessful, as did an aristocratic revolt in Russia five years later. Revolution bubbled to the surface again across Europe in 1830 and 1848. Most of these revolts were expressed in a distinctly French idiom that stressed written constitutions, individual rights, and national sovereignty and was broadcast loudly from the barricades. Long after 1815, France was a godparent to aspiring revolutionaries everywhere.

The Golden Age of Barricades

"It was the collaboration of the pavement, the block of stone, the beam, the bar of iron, the rag, the scrap, the broken pane, the unseated chair, the cabbage-stalk, the tatter, the rag, and the malediction. It was grand and it was petty. It was the abyss parodied on the public place by hubbub. The mass beside the atom; the strip of ruined wall and the broken bowl, threatening fraternization of every sort of rubbish. . . . [It was] the alluvium of revolt."

Victor Hugo's magnificent evocation of a Parisian barricade in *Les Misérables* (1862) helped cement its place in the nineteenth-century European imagination. This most elementary of tools of urban warfare is said to have originated during the Fronde in 1648, and barricades were used to block troops on a couple of occasions in the 1790s. But it was their use in the Paris uprisings of 1830, 1848, and 1871 that made them an icon of revolt.

Rebuilding after Napoleon

The congress of European powers that met in Vienna in 1815 had no time for the transnational language of revolution. Rather, they were determined to set the world to rights after its Napoleonic adventure, not least by snuffing out sparks of rebellion wherever they flared. They also saw to it that France no longer had the power base to support uprisings elsewhere. Its frontiers were fixed at their 1792 levels, though it was granted a few colonial crumbs, mainly trading posts in India and west Africa and a few former possessions in the Caribbean—without the former jewel in the crown that was now independent Haiti.

The French economy was powerfully affected by the loss of both empires, terrestrial and colonial. Overseas losses blighted the Atlantic coast ports that had once thrived on their Caribbean connection. On the other side of the Channel, England was well into its Industrial Revolution. France lagged far behind. Any effort to catch up was inhibited by a slowdown in population growth.

Coitus Interruptus

Nineteenth-century France had a population problem. For reasons that remain mysterious, the French began systematically using coitus interruptus several generations before other European states. An industrializing economy requires a large and elastic labor supply. While all of France's economic rivals achieved this, France's birth rate dropped after 1800. There was no technological reason for this: barrier methods of contraception only became generalized after 1870, notably following the vulcanization of rubber. Catholic apologists argued that the 1789 Revolution had deterred French men and women from following Catholic teaching on procreation. The more likely reason is Napoleonic land settlement. The choice of partible inheritance over primogeniture made restricting births an urgent necessity for peasants with large families to provide for.

Even the climate seemed to be conspiring to stunt France's economic recovery. The volcanic eruption of Mount Tambora in Indonesia in 1815 sent up enormous ash clouds that darkened the face of Europe the following year, producing the coldest summer on record. The world had to wait until the end of the millennium for another event on this scale, caused by the Hekla volcano in Iceland in 2000.

The July Monarchy

Waterloo and Mount Tambora combined to set the restored regime of the Bourbons off to a miserable start. The new king, Louis XVIII, had been absent from France since 1793 and was placed on his throne by European allies. In a spirit of compromise, he issued a "Constitutional Charter" with an elected assembly (though there were no Rights of Man and only a tiny minority of the elite had the vote). But his moderation was criticized by the frankly vengeful returned émigré nobility.

The latter felt their time had come in 1824. Louis's successor Charles X was a full-on supporter of the union of "throne and altar"—that is, the alliance of divine right monarchy with anti-modernising Catholicism. But public opinion had moved well beyond this kind of reactionary approach to governing. Charles's attempts to roll back electoral rights in the late 1820s led to further rebellion. The *Trois Glorieuses*—three days of Parisian revolt from July 27–29, 1830—had the king running for his life. A republic seemed to be waiting in the wings, but deft political footwork by the duke of Orléans, scion of a collateral branch of the Bourbons, saw him emerging as ruler. He took the title Louis-Philippe in what became known as the July Monarchy.

Louis-Philippe represented a firmer center ground in the political quagmire of the post-Napoleonic years. His father had

been a passionate supporter of the Revolutionary cause (though he had ended up on the guillotine) and the new king had himself served in the Revolutionary army before fleeing into exile in 1793. Thrust into power in 1830, he burnished his popularity by supporting individual rights,

The *tricolore* held aloft by the symbolic figure of Marianne in Delacroix's famous painting *Liberty Leading the People*, the painter's homage to the *Trois Glorieuses* of 1830 expanding the electorate, and accepting the tricolor emblem. Above all, however, he shunned the old nobility and rejected Bourbon and Bonapartist ostentation.

As "Citizen King," Louis-Philippe offered support to the propertied and business classes. His governments opened up trade, boosted the banking sector, and invested heavily in infrastructure, notably in the just-invented railways. His minister Guizot's catch-phrase was "Get rich!" (*Enrichissez-vous!*)

Railways helped to turn the coal- and iron-rich parts of northern and eastern France into one of the most heavily industrialized parts of the world. As in Britain, the Low Countries, and western Germany, the hidden environmental costs of these "dark Satanic mills" were not fully grasped at the time, but the effects of coal smoke on human health were all too evident, as was the social impact of industrial change on the lives of growing numbers of city-based workers.

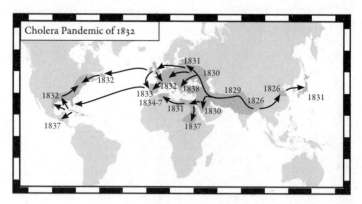

The 1832 cholera epidemic was a case of the empire striking back, the disease following colonial trade routes back to European cities. Contemporaries were not clear how cholera spread—germ theory would only emerge later in the century—but it was assumed the disease emerged from urban slums.

Working-class conditions were grim in emergent industrial cities like Saint-Etienne and Lille, as well as older centers such as Paris and Lyon. Paris of the 1830s was the city of Victor Hugo's novel *Les Misérables*, a place where poverty and radicalism rubbed promiscuous shoulders, producing an urban pathology into which a new pandemic, cholera, made a destructive entrance in 1832. Governments were well aware of "the social question," as it was called, but looked the other way. Their liberal ideology eschewed disturbing the workings of the free market. It was left to novelists and socialist writers to warn that cities were creating generations of "savages."

"Civilizing Mission"

During the 1820s and 1830s, a notion of France's "civilizing mission" began to emerge. It was directed less at "savage" industrial workers and more at "savages" in the wider world. Catholic missionary orders had long served as outriders for a French presence across the globe. But the mission now took on a secular aspect: it was no longer infidels and heretics to be converted, but the unenlightened. The idea was grounded in a belief in the superiority of France over other cultures and races, and the possibility of the improvement of humanity first debated in the Enlightenment.

A generation after France had lost one colonial empire, it now set its mind to creating another, with its civilizing mission as an ideological driver. The process got under way with the armed invasion of Algeria in 1830. What began as a punitive raid on Algiers soon widened into a full-blooded—and exceptionally bloody—colonising project.

Raising France's colonial profile was Louis-Philippe's way of rivaling Britain commercially, courting popularity at home, and also playing on Bonapartist sentiment. Europe's great powers had shut off the possibility of a repeat performance of the Napoleonic experiment, but so, too, had the peoples of Europe. Napoleon's destructive wars and a burning hostility toward French control had forged strong nationalist sentiment in Spain and Portugal, Russia, the Italian peninsula, and the fragmented collection of states within the German Confederation, heir to the Holy Roman Empire. Intellectuals who might once have been proud Jacobin sympathizers poured their energies into these emerging nationalist movements. Fired up with Romantic-era passion and pride, patriotic thinkers discovered a new affinity with their German- or English-speaking peers rather than francophone culture.

Yet France's soft power remained considerable. French cosmopolitanism had made its mark on Europe's capitals, while vestiges of imperial France—the Napoleonic civil code, the constitutions and the Rights of Man, the metric system—lingered in numerous states that had once been within the Napoleonic empire. After 1815, moreover, Paris became a refuge for waves of foreign political exiles, drawn to the birthplace of the barricade: Marx and Engels from Germany, the nationalist agitator Mazzini from Italy, and the anarchist Bakunin from Russia, among others, all keen to learn the insurrectionary trade at the feet of France's radical theorists and the heirs of the sans-culottes.

The power of French attraction proved particularly strong in the arts. Paris's École des Beaux-Arts taught Europe's painters how to paint, while the Louvre provided a model to which the world's best museums aspired. France's painters (Delacroix, Géricault, Ingres, Gros) as well as its poets (Victor Hugo, Lamartine, Baudelaire, Verlaine) and composers from Berlioz onward enjoyed European renown. The European realist novel originated in

France with Stendhal and was taken forward by Balzac's
astonishing multi-volume *Comédie humaine,* which explored
from high to low the nature of post-revolutionary society. The
French realists, including, later in the century, Flaubert and Zola,
reinvented the novel in ways that powerfully impacted the
imaginations of European readers. Revealingly, more nineteenth-
century European novels were set in Paris than in any other city.

Honoré de Balzac, surrounded by characters from his novels; drawing by
Jean-Jacques Grandville for reproduction on a fan

Despite this rich cultural influence, and for all its early promise,
the July Monarchy could only conjure an inescapable drabness that
made it difficult to love. Harvest failures and an industrial downturn in the late 1840s set off calls for political reform. When the
government tried to ban protests in February 1848, the barricades
were up in a flash and a revolution was in the offing.

"When France sneezes," the Austrian statesman Metternich remarked, "the rest of Europe catches a cold." And indeed within weeks of the Parisian flare-up, barricades were being erected in major cities across Europe, threatening to destabilize the conservative world created at the 1815 Congress of Vienna. The turbulence of 1848—evident in every European state except Russia and Britain—was to have a profound influence on the course of European history. In the case of France, it meant the overthrow of the July Monarchy and its replacement by a republic. The president of that Second Republic, elected in late 1848, had an ominous surname: Bonaparte.

CHAPTER 5

FRANCE'S GERMAN CENTURY
Europe, Empire, and Colonialism (1850–1940)

The course of French history in the century after the European revolutions of 1848 was dominated by two issues that loomed large beyond the borders of the Hexagon. The first of these was colonial empire. The second was Germany.

The final abolition of slavery in 1848 meant that further colonial expansion would be achieved on a different basis from France's first overseas empire. This point was taken on board by Napoleon's nephew Louis Napoleon Bonaparte, who became Emperor Napoleon III in 1852, as well as by the Third Republic (1870–1940) that followed him. France built the largest colonial empire of modern times after the British, containing nearly 10 percent of the world's population. While its vast territories added a global dimension to the country's cultural and civilizational prowess, expanding, administering, and holding on to them involved an enormous commitment of French energies.

The second, more intractable issue was closer to home. A process of German unification had begun in earnest after the 1848 revolutions under the aegis of the kingdom of Prussia, skilfully navigated by Bismarck. The master statesman engineered Prussia and its allies into a conflict—the Franco-Prussian war of 1870–1871—that would be Napoleon III's nemesis. A newly united Germany took as its spoils of war the partly German-speaking provinces of Alsace and Lorraine. Reclaiming those lost provinces and wreaking *la revanche* (revenge) on Germany within Europe became a headline item in French international policy that would eventually lead the country into two catastrophic global wars—in 1914 and then in 1939.

Empire or Republic?
Second Republic (1848–1852)
Second Empire (1852–1870)
Third Republic (1870–1940)

City of Light

Paris of the late nineteenth century developed a lasting reputation as the most civilized of world cities and the very acme of urban modernity. The process began with Louis Napoleon Bonaparte. Trading on the family name, he was elected president of the new Second Republic in 1848, before seizing power and assuming the mantle of president-for-life, and then of emperor. From the outset, Emperor Napoleon III worked hand-in-glove with Georges Haussmann, his Prefect of Paris, to undertake a wholesale remodeling of the French capital.

The new ruler committed himself to ending Paris's reputation as a breeding ground for disease, misery, and revolt. Instead, he would rebuild a new kind of modern city. He and Haussmann saw themselves as urban physicians prescribing a road to health for a sick and rebellious patient. They set about speeding up the city's circulatory system through the construction of boulevards. They created new parks and green space that cleansed the air Parisians breathed. They put in place an astonishing underground sewage system permitting hygienic removal of waste. And they demolished poor-quality housing, replacing it with swanky apartments.

Haussmann's 1850s template for Parisian housing blocks followed building regulations on height and width inherited from the eighteenth century. This gave the city center a reassuring sense of historical continuity.

Destroying working-class housing at the historic heart of the city had powerful political overtones, for these poorer neighborhoods were not only blamed for the cholera outbreaks that decimated Paris in the 1830s and 1840s but had also been seen as breeding grounds of popular radicalism since the days of the sans-culottes. Napoleon wanted to make central Paris safe for the bourgeoisie. Workers were dumped unceremoniously beyond the periphery, allowing the heart of the city to be populated by the wealthier classes who flocked to inhabit Haussmann's famous housing blocks.

An Imperial-Style Republic

Napoleon III's ignominious defeat, capture, and dethronement in 1871 threw the entire Haussmannian project into question. One might have expected the Third Republic to reject the Prefect's grandiose rebuilding plans, not least because they were borderline corrupt. Yet despite some misgivings among republicans,

Haussmann's vision was well established as the global template for a modern city. There was no turning back. More boulevards were constructed by the republic between 1871 and 1914 than under the previous imperial regime, and far more residential blocks were built in the style that Haussmann made famous. His urban model would go on to be copied throughout the French provinces and in the urban centers of France's expanding empire, from Algiers to Pondicherry and from Hanoi to Dakar. The characteristic Haussmannian style was also a powerful influence on countless cities across Europe and the Americas.

The Paris Commune

An attempt by Parisian radicals to revive the city's revolutionary tradition led to the so-called Paris Commune of 1871. But the Communards' mixture of anti-clerical and socialist ideas had little time to acquire national resonance. The provisional government sent in infantry troops to crush the movement with exceptional brutality.

Monument to the Victims of Revolutions by Paul Moreau-Vauthier: Located next to the Père Lachaise cemetery on Avenue Gambetta, it incorporates stones from the original *Mur des Fédérés*. Vauthier first achieved public renown as a sculptor at the universal exposition of 1900, the same year he designed the memorial.

In a bloody climax in the Père Lachaise cemetery, the last Communards were lined up and shot against the so-called *Mur des Fédérés*, which went on to become a pilgrimage site for the French left for generations. The incendiary fires that blazed in the movement's final days caused considerable damage to Haussmann's Paris. Many landmarks were burnt to the ground. Some, such as the Hôtel de Ville, the city hall, were restored from the ruins. Others, such as the Tuileries palace, never reemerged.

The Third Republic also adopted Napoleon III's practice of showcasing Paris to the world in *expositions universelles*, or world fairs. The first outstandingly successful version of a modern universal exposition had been London's Great Exhibition of 1851. It enthused the French emperor, who shamelessly adopted the idea wholesale for his own capital in 1855 and 1867. The Third Republic went one step further. In 1878, the republican regime used a universal exposition to show the world how it had put Paris back together again after the divisive and destructive episode of the Paris Commune.

Further expositions added to the built environment. The 1889 fair saw the construction of the Eiffel Tower and set a world record of thirty-two million attendees. The exposition of 1900 involved the creation of the Grand and Petit Palais exhibition spaces, the Alexandre III Bridge and the first Metro line. The event attracted over fifty million visitors. Some forty nations participated, each erecting a national pavilion to showcase their wares.

Nineteenth-century Paris was probably more painted—and painted in—than any city before or since. Though initially dismissed as mere "impressionists," the painters of modern life (as the poet Charles Baudelaire called them)—Monet, Cézanne,

Pissarro, Degas, Seurat, Renoir, Morisot, Caillebotte, Sisley, and others—made Paris and its boulevard life their subject matter. The city became a training ground for budding artists from all over the globe and the heart of the international art market. The emergence from the 1890s of photography as both a "high" art form and a humble hobby further raised the city's profile. Picture postcards—particularly profuse during the expositions—registered Paris firmly on French and international retinas.

In 1889, Gustav Eiffel placed on his eponymous iron tower the names not of kings and emperors, nor of artists and poets, but rather seventy-two outstanding French scientists, scholars, and engineers. The decision highlighted the Third Republic's emphasis on science, technology, and education and the role of the expositions in endorsing spectacular innovations and engineering feats. Cameras and Singer sewing machines were among the biggest hits of the 1855 expo, as were refrigerators, typewriters, and telephones in 1878.

The architect Hector Guimard designed over 150 subway entrances between 1900 and World War I, which popularized the *Art Nouveau* style. Around half survive and enjoy protected status.

The mass use of electricity in the 1900 world fair gave Paris the enduring nickname of the "City of Light." The same exposition outlined the shape of things to come in the twentieth century with moving sidewalks, diesel engines, electric cars, and cinema films. The Eiffel Tower divided aesthetic opinion, but Guimard's elegantly curvaceous *Art Nouveau* Métro entrances showed the world that peerless urban engineering could be ultra-stylish too.

The Third Republic invested heavily in higher education, giving Paris the additional accolade of a world city of science and research. Louis Pasteur's work on the sterilization of food and his anthrax and rabies vaccines won him considerable fame. The physiologist Claude Bernard, the physicists Marie and Pierre Curie, the neurologist Jean-Martin Charcot (Freud's mentor), and the mathematician Henri Poincaré also became celebrities. The enormously popular novelist Jules Verne caught the science bug and created a lasting vogue for science fiction.

A Trip to the Moon

The first movies made by the pioneering Lumière brothers in the late 1890s were films of everyday events, such as

 a train pulling into the station and workers leaving a factory. But before long, the film impresario Georges Méliès cashed in on the popular taste for science fiction. Full of trick photography and special effects, *Une Voyage à la lune* ("A Trip to the Moon") appeared in 1902.

If the Paris expositions highlighted French scientific high-mindedness, they also promoted entertainment and frivolity. Haussmann's city was more closely structured around leisure than work—which, like workers, was being pushed beyond the periphery of the old city walls. In the heart of the capital, the consumer ruled. Anyone with money in their pocket could enjoy the bright lights of Paris—the fabled cafés, bars, brasseries, restaurants, cabarets, theaters, music halls, and brothels (sexual services constituting a vibrant branch of the tourist industry). Though no one needed cash to behave as a *flâneur*, wandering the streets of the city and drinking in its sensations. Catering to a mass urban culture that prized the visually spectacular and thrilling, the universal expos resembled fun fairs more than scientific laboratories.

The Flâneur

Baudelaire: a self-portrait made under the influence of hashish (c. 1840)

Many cities lend themselves to aimless wandering, but nineteenth-century Paris was the birthplace of the *flâneur,* the "passionate spectator," whose "passion and profession are to become one flesh with the crowd," as Baudelaire declared in 1863. "For the perfect *flâneur* . . . it is an immense joy to set up house in the heart of the multitude, amid the ebb and flow of movement, in the midst of the fugitive and the infinite." Haussmann's modern city offered a new kind of social and literary identity, allowing the *flâneur*—and his female counterpart the *passante*, in Proust's parlance—an opportunity to be absorbed by the milling crowd.

"Europe has gone off to view the merchandise," one early critic of the expositions acerbically remarked. For the fairs, though fun, were also major commercial operations. The emergence of department stores along the lines of the *Galeries Lafayette* and *Au Bon Marché* had created new forms of impulse-driven shopping that the expositions exploited. Like them, they offered a captivating mix of desirable consumer objects and tourist bric-à-brac. They served to strengthen Paris's well-honed reputation for luxury and semi-luxury products—*haute couture*, jewelry, accessories, perfumes, and other must-haves. Mass demand also boosted the production of cheap knockoffs. *Articles de Paris,* as they were called, formed an important sector of French manufacturing.

Industrial Revival

In the first half of the century, French industry was left standing by British mechanized production. France fared rather better after 1850. Improvements in banking and credit facilities as well as gold discoveries in California and Australia led to a boom in global trade in the early 1850s. A spectacular railway boom boosted demand for rolling stock, rails, and coal, which in turn galvanized coal, steel, and iron production in France's industrializing north and east. French scientific and engineering prowess was better attuned to this so-called Second Industrial Revolution, which was dominated by the steel, aluminium, chemical, gas, and electricity industries and newer sectors such as bicycle, motor car, and movie production. Many of these required state investment and the kind of technical expertise that resonated strongly with the French tradition of *dirigisme*.

Climatic conditions finally began to improve in the 1850s. Alpine glaciers started to recede, for reasons that remain unclear, though the process may have been aggravated late in the century by high levels of industrial soot. But any advantage farming might have gained from the milder climate was countered by an economic depression from the 1870s to the 1890s. Southern departments at first benefited from the arrival of the railways, which put northern wine-drinkers within easy reach. However, vine-killing outbreaks of phylloxera ravaged the industry from the 1870s. Characteristically, French scientists found the solution: grafts from American vine stocks.

Overall, however, the picture was far from gloomy. Life expectancy was on the rise—from around thirty years in 1850 to almost forty by 1914—as were general living standards. Bread and wine

The success of the Paris universal expositions spawned a host of similar shows in provincial cities, such as here in Nice.

consumption rose by 50 percent. Meat, beer, and cider expenditure doubled, alcohol consumption tripled, and sugar and coffee use quadrupled. There were spectacular increases in spending on newsprint, leisure, and sporting activities. Tourism was also on the rise: the Côte d'Azur, made easily accessible by rail, became a destination of choice for city dwellers. An impressive postal system allowed department store catalogs and Parisian fancy goods and commodities to reach remote doorsteps. The author Charles Péguy claimed in 1914 that French society had changed more since the 1880s than it had in the whole period dating back to the Romans. He was exaggerating, of course, but not by much.

Building a New Empire

For most French men and women, these improvements in daily life owed much to the global trade links that France had been gradually rebuilding over the century. Colonizing impulses were well served by a global revolution in communications. French investment in ventures such as the Trans-Siberian Railway and the Orient Express internationalized the French rail network. Electric telegraph connected not just cities but entire continents. Steamships cut global journey times by sea dramatically, all the more so after the inauguration of the Suez Canal in 1869, which marked a huge boost to France's engineering prestige as well as its overseas trade.

The Suez Canal was a real achievement for Napoleon III. Yet the emperor was a ditherer in colonial affairs. He was full of big ideas for boosting France's global prestige, but most failed to ignite. Grandiose plans to turn the Mediterranean into a "French Sea" came to nothing, while military intervention in Mexico in the 1860s was an embarrassing fiasco. In practice, he preferred to build an informal empire by connecting spheres of economic influence in the Caribbean, West Africa, Madagascar, the Near East, East Asia, and New Caledonia and Oceania generally. Only where Napoleon encountered substantial local resistance—as with New Caledonia in 1853–1854 and Cochin-China (including much of Vietnam) in the 1860s—did he move from informal influence to outright annexation.

The Algerian Experiment

Algeria was a case in point. Napoleon III initially dismissed the troublesome colony as a "ball and chain round France's ankle." He even toyed with forming a semi-autonomous Arab monarchy under French mentorship. Yet during visits to North Africa in the 1860s, he began to visualize Algeria's potential as a kind of colonial laboratory and settlement zone. This area of French occupation had been formed into departments in 1848, as though it was merely Corsica with added sand. The emperor experimented with various methods of colonial development, building railways, providing incentives for agrarian projects, and introducing French legal and administrative structures.

Without exception, however, these gifts of empire favored settlers from France over the indigenous population. As resistance to French authority grew, Napoleon adopted a more directly interventionist approach. The emperor authorized the creation of settler villages and the confiscation of indigenous lands in a massive land grab. Prolonged periods of rebellion met with a brutal response. Atrocity piled upon atrocity and massacre upon massacre, in an orgy of violence unimaginable in neighboring Europe. The native Algerian population fell by as much as a third between 1830 and 1875 due to warfare, disease, and starvation.

The "pacification" of Algeria continued into the following century, as did the systematic favoring of colonial settlers. After Napoleon III's fall, immigration widened to include significant contingents from Italy and Spain. By 1914, colonists numbered nearly a million. The army's presence enabled the use of the indigenous population as forced labor in many areas of economic life.

Emir Abdelkader

Abd al-Qadir al-Hassani al-Jaza'iri, or Emir Abdelkader (1808–1883), was a Muslim religious leader and resistance fighter who is venerated as an Algerian national hero. From the early 1830s, he united tribes in western Algeria against the French, establishing a large powerbase there. After eventually surrendering in 1847, he spent time in French prisons before being allowed to live in exile. Throughout the wars of resistance, he consistently showed humane treatment of Europeans, and while in exile in 1860, he acted to prevent Christians in Damascus from massacre. This was in contrast to France's brutal repression of Algerian rebels and indeed its general treatment of Muslims. An important ruling in 1865 stipulated that Muslims had to renounce their faith to become French citizens. Religion, or at least their religion, was felt to be incompatible with the secularist principles of the Revolution.

Race and the Republic

It might seem odd for the Third Republic, which prided itself on championing the democratic values of the 1789 Declaration of the Rights of Man, to embrace colonialism quite so enthusiastically. But it increasingly justified the imperial project it inherited from

Napoleon III in terms of "inferior races."

The study of human diversity had emerged from the Enlightenment with many good intentions. But in the early nineteenth century a fad for comparative anatomy was used to give spurious scientific backing to racist beliefs and other ingrained prejudices. The dissections performed by the scientist Georges Cuvier on "Hottentot" women notorious for the size of their buttocks led him to conclude that they were anatomically closer to apes than humans. This opened the door to the pseudoscience of race.

The idea of a hierarchy of races with white "Caucasian Man" poised triumphantly at its apex became commonplace in the nineteenth century. Craniometry, the measurement of human skulls and brains, was used to reinforce the notion that the "lower races" were mentally and morally as well as physically inferior. Notions of white male supremacy were further bolstered by

Kanak village, *Exposition Universelle*, Paris 1889

specious extrapolations from the evolutionary ideas of Jean-Baptiste Lamarck and Charles Darwin. What universalist republicans took to be science made it possible for them to accept the inferiority of colonized peoples—pending the effects of the civilizing mission to bring them up to European standards.

The Paris expositions gave racism an eminent platform. Napoleon III had recognized their potential for popularizing the colonial project among a still-skeptical general public. His 1855 and 1867 shows presented French zones of influence in Algeria and the wider world in the rosiest light. In 1867, there were specific colonial pavilions for certain territories, often in indigenous architectural styles and displaying local manufactured goods. The Third Republic followed his lead. In 1878, an oriental bazaar was set up for North African artisans, turning parts of Paris into "Marrakech-sur-Seine."

A "black village" inhabited by imported Africans was also created in 1878 to complement displays of local goods and practices. By 1900, this popular feature had been expanded to include indigenous peoples from northern and sub-Saharan Africa, along with "colonial natives" from East Asia, New Caledonia, and Oceania. Public displays of belly-dancing and casual female nudity added an erotic frisson to the shows. In what were effectively human zoos, white Westerners viewed their "inferiors" like wild animal species in their "natural" habitat—and congratulated themselves on their own superiority.

The Scramble for Africa

The 1889 and 1900 expositions also bore witness to France's switch from informal empire to formal annexation. In the so-called Scramble for Africa, ratified by the Berlin Conference

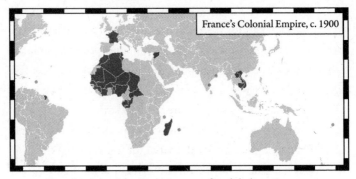

France's Colonial Empire, c. 1900

French territorial gains in its quest for global empire were
greatest in northern and western Africa.

of 1884–1885, the main European powers divided up the African
continent among themselves.

France laid claim to huge expanses of northern, western,
and equatorial Africa, and strengthened its grip on Madagascar.
License to annex was practiced on a global scale: France also made
major gains in Indochina and across Oceania. The settlement
model of colonization favored in Algeria was, however, abandoned. The new economic logic was predatory and extractive,
based on siphoning off resources and developing the colonies as
outlets for French trade.

In addition to the great Paris expositions, successful colonial
exhibitions in provincial towns such as Rouen in 1896, Rochefort in
1898, and Marseille in 1906 helped to drum up popular support for
the colonial project. Human zoos stimulated coverage in the popular
press. Similarly, a booster literature of expo guides and pamphlets,
adventure stories, and travel literature played strongly on national
and racial stereotypes. They offered a fig leaf to the civilizing mission,
occluding the raw violence involved in colonial expansion as well
as the destruction of indigenous cultures. The effect was to make
French colonialism seem an integral element of French nationalism.

The Making of a Nation

In 1882, the influential scholar and ardent republican Ernest Renan gave a lecture at the Sorbonne on "What is a nation?" He rejected the idea that divine right of rulers, racial purity, linguistic unity, religious homogeneity, historical prescription, or mere tradition could form its basis.

> A nation's existence is a daily plebiscite. It presupposes a past but is reiterated in the present by a tangible fact: consent, the clearly expressed desire to continue a common life.

It was a timely sentiment for a more democratic age. The 1870 constitution had reinstated universal male suffrage. The very existence of a modern state, it seemed, depended on what people thought of it—or at least white men, since colonial subjects and women were still denied the vote. It was also a time of rising nationalism in Germany, Italy, and more broadly across the Austro-Hungarian and Ottoman empires. The emergence of strong nation-states marked a significant shift in international relations. Rather than rely on the collective security mechanisms in play since 1815, the great powers made alliances among themselves. Two armed camps developed, pitting Germany, Austria, and Italy against France and its allies, Russia, and, after an *entente cordiale* in 1905, Britain.

At the heart of this golden age of nationalism was the issue of political community. Higher literacy rates and the growth of a mass audience for print fostered what Benedict Anderson dubbed "imagined communities"–resilient networks of individuals tied together by more than face-to-face contact. In order for governments to win their "daily plebiscite," even stronger bonds of loyalty toward governing elites had to be forged. Supporters of the Third Republic from the 1870s onward were acutely conscious that the state needed to inspire support, affection, and commitment.

There were hearts and minds aplenty to be won over to the idea of a republic. Yet it was, in the words of the wily politician Adolphe Thiers, "the regime that divides us the least." Bonapartist populism was in tatters following the 1870–1871 defeat, the radical left was utterly discredited by the Paris Commune experience, while the royalist right was proving unacceptably reactionary and divisive. The Third Republic largely owed its early survival to the manifest incompetence of its opponents.

From unpromising beginnings, the politicians of the new republic fashioned a regime that lasted almost as long—seventy years—as all those since 1789 put together. They did this by adopting a pragmatic approach that stressed the art of the politically possible. Hedging, fudging, compromising, and cutting deals were the order of the day. While it sometimes strayed into outright corruption, this flexible behavior bought the republican regime a degree of support that was all the more remarkable given the turbulence on the wider international landscape. Dewy-eyed monarchists, Bonapartist nostalgists, and leftists dreaming of the Jacobin victories of the 1790s rallied behind the nationalist project.

Third Republic politicians viewed overseas expansion as fundamental to French nationhood. The colonial champion Jules Ferry held that the "higher races have a right over the lower races," adding that "they have a duty to civilize." France's colonial mission would be about bringing freedom, higher standards, and a better way of life to the less fortunate, not oppression or exploitation as was the case with other nations. Or so French colonialists told themselves.

Resetting the Republic

A female profile representing either Marianne or the fertility goddess Ceres first appeared on French postage stamps in 1849 under the Second Republic.

The French people needed to be taught the values of colonialism, but also the value of the Republic. The Rights of Man prefaced the 1870 constitution and the tricolor was confirmed as the national flag. In 1879, the Marseillaise was adopted as the national anthem. The next year, Bastille Day was made an annual national holiday. Busts of Marianne, red-bonneted symbol of the revolutionary republic since the 1790s, began to appear in town halls across the empire, replacing those of Napoleon III. From around 1900, her image started to appear on coins, often as a sower, with postage stamps to follow.

Politicians used the education system to impart their vision of the *République française*. Laws introduced by Jules Ferry in the 1880s made primary education compulsory throughout France—a huge step for any nation. Related reforms supported teacher training, enhanced the secondary schools (*lycées*) created by Napoleon, and improved girls' education.

The Spirit of Revenge

The teaching of history in Third Republic schools recast France's civilizing mission as a secular project, minimizing the church's role in the Crusades while playing down French involvement in slavery and the slave trade. The

Terror was framed as a patriotic moment par excellence when the nation in arms faced down the massed armies of European *anciens régimes*—led by the Germanic Holy Roman Empire. Schooling also sought to inculcate the spirit of *la revanche* against Germany for seizing Alsace and Lorraine in 1870. Indeed, "Barbarian Germany" was painted as an even more mendacious long-term enemy of French interests and values than Perfidious Albion. In these ways, hatred of Germany over the 1870–1871 defeat and the Alsace-Lorraine issue was normalized and given historical justification.

To win popular support, the political elite felt it needed to communicate effectively with all corners of the Republic. Yet on the eve of 1870, French was still not spoken in roughly a quarter of French communes. Politicians took their cue from the 1790s. The First Republic had seen French as "the language of liberty" and viewed other tongues as backward-looking, tied to clerical and localist values, and incompatible with a "united and indivisible" republic.

An attack on illiteracy in the classroom was conducted in French, which was held to be the "mother language" of all French boys and girls. Children who were heard speaking other languages or dialects were shamed and humiliated. French was similarly made the language of all instruction in the colonies, where indigenous children were also, comically, expected to respect "their ancestors the Gauls."

Like their Revolutionary forebears, Third Republic politicians viewed the Catholic Church as a major obstacle to the formation of good republicans. As the leading politician Léon Gambetta

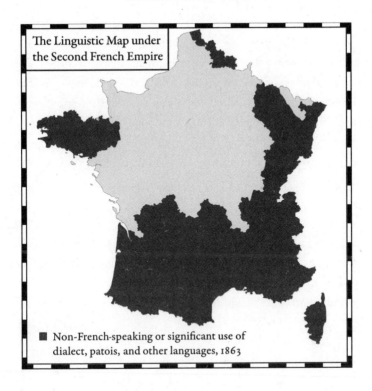

The Linguistic Map under the Second French Empire

Non-French-speaking or significant use of dialect, patois, and other languages, 1863

put it, *Le cléricalisme, voilà l'ennemi!* ("Clericalism, that's the enemy!") Statesman Jules Ferry meanwhile demanded "schools without God." The Third Republic had discovered the value of laicity (*laïcité*), a term destined for notoriety a century later that meant ridding public institutions of any form of religious influence. Public space was to be kept neutral to allow the inculcation of secular republican values in the spirit of the 1790s. The point was underlined by the formal separation of church and state in 1905.

The Republic applied a similar nationalist spirit to French citizenship. The year 1789 had established the universalist notion of the citizen, endowed with equal rights guaranteed by the state.

From 1848, this guarantee was extended to enfranchised ex-slaves, but the position was very different in non-slave colonies. The settlement model of colonization in Algeria produced a two-tier society. European incomers were given citizenship and a vote, while indigenous Algerians could only count on the protection of the state without political rights. An Indigenous Code for Algeria in 1881 gave French bureaucrats powers that were both sweeping and arbitrary in all administrative and legal matters.

The Black Man's Burden

The costs of empire proved surprisingly small for the state—less than 1 percent of France's gross domestic product. Much of that was spent on the army, although most of the overall cost of the military and colonial administration was borne by the colonized,

A large percentage of troops in the colonies were in fact local recruits. Following the creation of the Foreign Legion in 1831, the North African *zouaves* (infantry) and *spahis* (light cavalry, shown above near Furnes in Belgium in 1914) were formed in the 1830s and 1840s, and the *tirailleurs sénégalais* (Senegalese riflemen), drawn from across western Africa, in 1857. These formations went on to fight throughout the empire and in both world wars.

in the form of taxes of one sort or another. In France's African colonies, colonization was very much the "Black Man's Burden."

Most colonies acquired in the late nineteenth century were not regarded as suitable for mass European settlement. For them the state developed a protectorate-like system, with a small number of French officials ruling over societies of millions, many of whose inhabitants would never catch sight of a French man or woman. As in Algeria, the colonial establishment protected the civic and political rights of the privileged few who enjoyed citizen status. From 1887, the vast majority of colonial subjects were placed under indigenous codes on the Algerian model.

Medicine and Empire

The Pasteur Institute for medical research in Paris was founded in 1888 and named after the great scientist. It set up colonial branches in Cochin-China (1891), North Africa (1894), Madagascar (1898), and later in Dakar and Guadeloupe (both in 1924). Medical provision high-lighted France's two-tier approach to empire, however. The institutes tended to focus on disease prevention for European colonizers rather than the broader health challenges of the colonized.

While happy to restrict citizen rights in its colonies, the Republic maintained a liberal policy on the integration of foreigners within the Hexagon. A naturalization law introduced in 1851 was strengthened in 1889 to extend full rights of citizenship to children born in France to immigrants. The main beneficiaries— Italian, Spanish, Belgian, and Swiss—were European newcomers. The welcoming approach was motivated by the premature fall in

French births. This was all the more worrying given the rapid population growth rates of other industrializing nations. France's population grew by less than 10 percent between 1871 and 1911; its great rival Germany's rose by an ominous 60 percent.

The relatively liberal approach to immigration faced a substantial challenge from the 1880s, as Ashkenazi Jews began arriving as a result of antisemitic pogroms in Russia and eastern Europe. Around 100,000 of these refugees were established by 1914, a large proportion of them in Paris. This was very much the moment in the history of modern France that immigration began to be perceived as "the immigration problem."

The key question for the Republic was integration. Could immigrants be willing and active members of Renan's voluntary national community? Rather than birthplace or bureaucratic formality, the litmus test was now behavior. Although committed to integration within France, many Jewish newcomers were keen to retain their Yiddish language and culture. Pseudoscientific racial profiling complicated the issue, with the Ashkenazim held to constitute an "inferior" race. Laïcité also seemed at stake. Anticlerical republicans regarded deeply held religious views as an impediment to true patriotism—as many Catholics and Muslims already knew to their cost.

The right-wing popular press inflamed the mood. Jeremiads about immigration dropped in accusations that the republic was in thrall to Jewish moneymakers and bankers. This anti-capitalist, antisemitic note struck a chord with many working people, for whom immigrants were rivals on the job market. The right had previously been dominated by reactionary Catholic aristocratic and landowning families. It now started to attract a mass following. Right-wing groups such as the *Action française* developed a penchant for street fighting. By the turn of the century, the right had been regenerated and given a populist orientation trading in antisemitic and xenophobic tropes.

Antisemitism became a neuralgic point in French politics with the so-called Dreyfus affair of 1894–1906, a miscarriage of justice carried out by the reactionary military establishment on a Jewish army officer, Albert Dreyfus, accused of spying for the Germans. This wrong was eventually righted, starting in 1898, when the

A Jew from Alsace, Alfred Dreyfus (1859–1935) joined the French army following the German assimilation of his homeland in the Franco-Prussian war. He bore the trumped-up case against him with some equanimity, despite a spell in the prison colony of Devil's Island in Guyana (where he is pictured above in 1898). Modest and unassuming, he volunteered to rejoin the army in 1914 at the age of 55 and fought at the battle of Verdun in 1916.

novelist Emile Zola made a famous, full-blooded attack on Dreyfus's persecutors in his article "*J'accuse*," published in *L'Aurore*, the newspaper edited by the radical politician Georges Clemenceau.

The Dreyfusard cause was led by the League of the Rights of Man, a new lobbying group that helped to resolve the affair through Dreyfus's pardon and reintegration into the army. But the episode came to be viewed worldwide as a lasting symbol of injustice. It also marks a significant moment in French history, when the language of the Rights of Man was reinstated within republican ideology with greater prominence.

The Rights of Men

In the decade following the Dreyfus affair, the League of the Rights of Man continued to champion rights issues, highlighting the prejudicial treatment of peoples living under French colonial rule, as well as the inferior position of women within France.

Olympe de Gouges's clarion call for the rights of women in the 1790s echoed through the nineteenth century, but it remained a cry in the wilderness. The highly patriarchal Code Napoléon set the clock back for women, keeping them confined in the home, subject to their fathers' or husbands' will. Staunch republicans resisted the extension of political rights to their wives and daughters. As women were more religious than men, it was claimed they would be vulnerable to manipulation by priests to vote for the Catholic right. Calls for a higher birth rate pointed in the same direction: women should stay at home and have babies. Unsurprisingly, given this stifling atmosphere, French suffragists struggled to make any gains before 1914.

Another area of injustice highlighted by the League was the rights of workers. Third Republic politicians showed little interest in the very real social problems that had been triggered by industrialization. Social security and welfare provision in France lagged way behind that in Germany and England. Poor working conditions, twelve-hour days, and a chronic lack of protection were the rule in the factories that now dominated France's manufacturing base.

As it emerged from its post-Commune slump, the militant left sought to change the agenda. In 1896, a trade union confederation, the CGT (*Confédération générale du travail*) was created and swiftly set about organizing major strikes. Though union protests had been legal since 1882, the government met them head-on, seeming to regard them as on a par with a recent spate of anarchist bomb-throwing. As interior minister from 1906, Clemenceau prided himself on being *le premier flic de France* ("France's top cop") and knocking heads together. In response to police violence, organized labor linked arms with radical left-wing parties. Yet by 1914, working-class pressure had forced some concessions that included accident insurance, a shorter working day, and retirement provision.

Rising Tensions

With tensions rising among the Great Powers, some working-class militants became disenchanted with national politics altogether. They renounced the *revanchiste* obsessions of mainline republicans and advocated community and even pacifism over jingoistic war-mongering. The red flag of internationalism, not the tricolor, floated over their rallies. In 1913, the left vigorously opposed attempts to extend the period of military conscription from two years to three. In the same year, the CGT resolved that if war broke out its members should not fight. The Socialist leader Jean Jaurès pleaded with the government to pull back from the brink and sought to organize a general strike on the issue. Domestic issues threatened to hobble the regime's freedom of action abroad.

The international arena was by now dangerously fraught. As a sign of the changing times, several global conflicts—notably the Philippine-American war (1899–1902), the Sino-Japanese war (1894–1895) and the Russo-Japanese war (1905)—now involved non-European actors. The European powers continued to indulge in saber-rattling across the globe. As late as 1898, Britain and France almost went to war over a military standoff in Sudan, in the village of Fashoda. In central Asia, Britain and Russia were locked in the so-called Great Game, while in the Balkans, Russia vied with Germany and Austria to support embryonic nation-states emerging from the crumbling Ottoman Empire.

It was in the Balkans that the spark for a general conflagration began, with the assassination in 1914 of Archduke Franz Ferdi-nand of Austria. Europe's two armed camps—France, Britain, and Russia on one side; Austria-Hungary, Germany, and Italy on the other—rolled ineluctably into war. It was a war that would change everything.

The Toils and Spoils of War (1914–1919)

For a country that seemed to be falling apart at the seams, the dec-laration of war produced a less brutal shock than was feared. The assassination, just days before, of the Socialist leader Jaurès by a student activist removed the only figure who might have mobi-lized workers against the war. Yet it seemed more popular than predicted, most people assuming any conflict would be short and sweet. Parliament was measured and unified in its response too, with the establishment of a Sacred Union (*L'Union sacrée*) of all parties supporting the war effort.

The regime almost came unstuck straight away. Germany attacked France through Belgium, advancing rapidly toward striking distance of Paris. But the Germans were driven back toward the frontier. Lines of trenches within French borders soon set out a battlefront extending from Dunkirk to the Franco-Swiss frontier. The great powers had anticipated a rapid war of movement along Napoleonic lines. What they got instead was a stultifying war of position on the western front. For the next four years, both sides made sporadic efforts to break through enemy lines. All resulted in failure—and huge casualties.

———— Front Line 1916–1917

– – – German withdrawal to Hindenburg line, March–April 1917

The most significant German assault was an attempt in 1916 to break through at Verdun. This was a site of republican memory.

Heroic French resistance here in 1792 had helped stop the Prussian advance on Paris. Now, the French under Marshal Pétain threw everything into their defense at enormous cost: the overall casualties were around three quarters of a million killed and wounded, equally shared between the two sides.

The strain of successive defiant but relentless campaigns began to tell at the front. In 1917, Pétain was obliged to deal with a number of mutinies. These appeared all the more worrying in the wake of the Bolshevik revolution, which dragged Russia out of its Franco-British-Russian alliance. Losses impacted morale on the home front too, where tensions were showing. Mobilization for war massively disrupted the economy and put severe pressure on civilian lives. Taxes and borrowing kept state finance afloat, but to the detriment of living standards. The state imposed itself powerfully on the economy, fixing prices, introducing rationing, and directing labor. As time dragged on, wartime restrictions led to defeatist talk and pacifist sentiments.

As it turned out, the country rallied under the powerful figure of Clemenceau, who emerged as a providential leader somehow above party strife. The "Tiger," as he

Clemenceau triumphant, November 11, 1918

was called, was ferociously committed to a final, unremitting push toward victory. This was achieved, partly due to wavering German morale, partly thanks to the United States joining the Franco-British alliance in 1917. Armistice with Germany was signed on November 11, 1918. Seven months later, Clemenceau and other leaders signed the Treaty of Versailles, which redrew the map of Europe.

The Propaganda War

Throughout the war, anti-German sentiment acted as an ideological glue for French soldiers and civilians alike. Government propaganda and posters stressed that the nation was fighting a war for humanity against not simply barbarians (as school textbooks had it), but savages worse than savages, troops who permitted themselves every imaginable atrocity. Accordingly there was a triumphant sense in 1919 that *la revanche* had been achieved at Versailles: Germany had been defeated and Alsace and Lorraine restored to France.

The war was won and lost on the Western Front, but France's empire played a significant role in the victory. Civilian manpower from the colonies proved an invaluable wartime resource, compensating for French workers sent to the front: 130,000 North Africans, 50,000 Indochinese, and a small contingent from Madagascar worked mainly in war factories alongside women, who were brought into the workforce en masse. The military contribution was even more striking: nearly six hundred thousand French colonial troops were deployed, around half of them from North Africa.

At the war's end, Germany was forced to renounce its own colonies, and its possessions were shared among the victors. In Africa, Togoland and part of the Cameroons came under French control, while France also benefited from the breakup of the Ottoman empire by the establishment of mandates in Syria and Lebanon.

The price of these gains was shockingly high. Apart from the utter destruction of the landscape along the Western Front, the most striking damage was demographic. Alsace and Lorraine brought 1.7 million individuals back into France. But the country had lost 1.4 million lives to the war. This was the highest proportion of any of the major combatants. Over a quarter of men aged eighteen to twenty-seven were dead. Casualty statistics for colonial troops were similarly brutal, while around two hundred thousand French civilians were killed. More than three

Monument to the victims of WWI in the commune of Goudelin in Brittany: It is said that just one of France's 36,000 communes escaped having any of its inhabitants killed in World War I. Over 95 percent have a memorial to their war dead. Poignantly, most were built at the prompting of local survivors of the conflict, paying homage to fallen comrades, family, and friends.

million men were left disabled, around a third of them permanently removed from the workforce, the destructive, mutilating impact of modern warfare on the human body would be visible on French streets for generations.

The war was ended by international alliance and the world was reshaped by international treaty. On the prompting of President Woodrow Wilson, the League of Nations was established with the aim of preventing warfare around the world. Yet any hope that this new spirit of internationalism would muzzle national aggression was misplaced. France saw the Versailles conference of 1919–1920 as a means of exacting a heavy price from Germany. The toll was already onerous. Germany had a higher overall number of war casualties than any nation and it had ceded territory to Belgium, Denmark, and Poland, as well as lost its overseas territories. But this was not enough for Clemenceau. He pushed for a stiff program of reparation payments, ignoring the grim economic state in which Weimar Germany now found itself.

Reparations proved an enduring apple of discord that fed German nationalism. In 1933, Hitler's Nazis were swept to power on the promise of destroying the Treaty of Versailles. By then, the United States had turned inward to its own affairs, robbing the League of Nations of most of its credibility. The interwar period felt uncomfortably like the period before 1914. The biggest international problem that still preoccupied European politicians was Franco-German antagonism. And if the French thought the country's German problem had been solved, they were very much mistaken.

From Versailles to Vichy (1919–1940)

The Spanish influenza pandemic of 1918–1919 caused more than two hundred thousand deaths in France alone, delaying recovery from the war. Its causes and rapid global spread owed much to the population movements caused by mobilization and then demobilization. Despite this setback, the pressures of war forced many sectors of heavy industry to modernize. This soon began to pay off. Industrial production was back at prewar levels as early as 1924 and 40 percent ahead by 1929. Iron, steel, automobile, and aircraft production all performed impressively.

France's colonies had generally proved their worth in the conflict, while their economic potential was widely appreciated. Although the cost of running the empire rose slightly, especially in the 1930s, it was still remarkably cheap. The discovery of oil in parts of the Middle East under French and English mandate was fortuitous, given the rise of the automobile and air travel. The extractive economic model of empire from the previous century

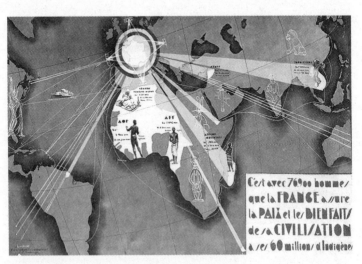

"It is with 76,900 men that France assures peace and the benefits of her civilization to her 60 million natives": a poster depicting the French *mission civilisatrice* from the 1931 Paris exposition.

continued. Efforts to grow other colonial industries—notably rubber—were given lower priority than French manufactures. The scale of assimilating an empire now some twenty times the size of metropolitan France looked increasingly daunting.

Public opinion after 1919 was probably more overtly pro-colonial in its views than ever before. Support extended further into the ranks of the left. While criticizing the aggressive use of violence by the colonial powers, the socialist leader Léon Blum even praised France's "civilizing mission." Long-established pro-colonial tropes were given a spectacular airing at the Colonial Exposition in Paris in 1931. Its director, Marshal Lyautey, claimed it as "a great work of peace," inspired by the mission of "winning over to human gentleness fierce hearts from the savanna or the desert."

The 1931 exposition reflected a more general scholarly and cultural interest in other cultures. Teaching and research in colonial studies were expanding at a number of Paris-based institutions, including the natural history museum and the *Musée ethnographique* (renamed the *Musée de l'homme* in 1937). The latter was the beneficiary of the huge state-organized Dakar-Djibouti expedition of 1931–1933, which crossed Africa from west to east, recording the impact of European influence on local societies. It also amassed a sizeable collection of cultural artifacts for the museum, adding to the African and Oceanic masks that had so inspired Picasso and Matisse and nurturing a cult of "negro art" among collectors. As ever, the colonial quest for knowledge shaded imperceptibly into outright plunder.

This point was made in protests at the Colonial Exposition in 1931. A number of members of the Surrealist artistic and literary movement issued a pamphlet titled, "Don't Visit the Colonial

Exposition." A counter-exhibition was held to tell "The Truth about the Colonies." As its organizers pointed out, the expo's director, Lyautey, had commanded French forces in the Rif War of 1924–1926 in Morocco, repressing rebels with considerable violence, while his Spanish allies in the conflict had used chemical warfare against civilians.

The impact of the Surrealist show was tiny, its five thousand visitors comparing poorly with the eight million who flocked to the official exposition. But the episode marked a significant change in attitudes. The Surrealists' anti-colonial stance was also shared by the French Communist Party. The communists were still small in numbers—they achieved only 12 deputies out of 605 returned in the 1932 elections—and most of their policies derived from Moscow. But they had opposed the colonial project from their earliest days. In fact, a founding member of the party was the future Vietnam resistance leader, Ho Chi Minh.

City of Exiles

In the early 1920s, Ho Chi Minh had lived close to the Place d'Italie in southeastern Paris, only a few hundred yards away from the cheap hotel room then occupied by Zhou Enlai, future Chinese leader and acolyte of Mao Zedong. In the 1930s, Léopold Senghor, independent Senegal's first president, and the leading Martiniquais intellectual André Césaire also lived in Paris during their studies. Together, they developed the theory of *Négritude* that would serve as a liberationist creed in francophone Africa and the French Caribbean. Paris's customary air of intellectual freedom and its reputation as a place of exile for the world's radicals and revolutionaries made it a congenial setting in which to dream of resistance.

Josephine Baker and Jazz

Founded in Paris in 1937, the Negritude movement valorized black and African cultural heritage and rejected both colonialism and the overt racism of the Nazi and Fascist movements. Its writers and artists were influenced by the ideas and works of French-based Surrealists and the Harlem Renaissance movement in Manhattan, as well as by jazz, which had established a strong foothold in Paris after 1918. Rather than return home, many African American soldiers had stayed on in the city after the war, musicians among them playing a leading role in the interwar jazz scene. The Negritude movement took on a global dimension as a result of the diaspora of black writers, artists, and musicians from Paris caused by World War II.

Josephine Baker is awarded the *Vermilion* medal of the city of Paris on March 3, 1956.

The singer, dancer, actress, nightclub performer, and all-around star entertainer Josephine Baker (1891–1975) came to symbolize the *années folles* of Paris in the 1920s. She became a French national in 1937. Born in Missouri and descended from enslaved and indigenous Americans, Baker went on to fashion an extraordinary career for herself that went well beyond the stage. She would be decorated for her work in the Resistance during Word War II, while her postwar civil rights activism spilled back into the United States, where she worked with Martin Luther King Jr. In 2021, she was inducted into the Pantheon, the first black woman to receive the honor—and certainly the first former headline act from the Folies Bergère.

Beneath the glitzy veneer, sluggish population growth continued to be an acutely French problem. Liberal rules on nationality, reinforced in 1927, encouraged the number of foreigners in France to double between the 1911 and 1931 censuses. Foreign-born residents now made up an even larger share of the French population than in the "melting pot" of the United States. The postwar demand for labor in France was largely answered by fellow Europeans—Italians foremost, but also Spaniards, Belgians, Poles, and Greeks. By contrast, the colonial laborers imported for the war effort were forced to go home, while women were also demobilized and pressured to return to the domestic front.

An economic downturn from 1931 put further pressure on foreigners, as ripples continued to spread from the Great Depression. With businesses collapsing, industry struggling, and unemployment high, jobs became scarce. Resentment at competition from immigrants was exploited by far-right parties, now reinforced with paramilitary wings and imported Fascist and Nazi ideas as well as home-grown xenophobia. A 1932 law instituting work visa quotas for different foreign communities was extended to the liberal professions in 1933. Both measures treated non-Europeans particularly harshly.

The Gathering Storm

It was the wave of Jewish immigrants fleeing Germany after the 1933 Nazi takeover that most incensed the far right. Antisemites denigrated the government as soft on Jews and foreigners, overly generous to the poor, and notoriously corrupt to boot. The corruption charge was certainly true, as covert deals between deputies and industrialists were legion. Protest over one such figure, the Ukrainian-Jewish businessman Alexandre Stavisky, triggered a far-right street demonstration in Paris in February 1934, in which armed protestors nearly overran the National Assembly. The government fell as a result.

Gathering storm clouds abroad—Hitler's aggression, Mussolini's campaign to conquer Ethiopia, and the deepening Spanish Civil War—further darkened the domestic mood. Left-wing groups mobilized to form a united front against the Fascist challenge at home. Nudged by the Soviet Union, the Communist Party distanced itself from some of its own rhetoric to adopt hypernationalistic positions.

In the legislative election campaign of 1936, Socialists, Communists, and other left-wing allies won a sizeable majority as the "Popular Front," brandishing the slogan "Bread, Peace, Freedom." Uncertainty followed hard on the heels of victory, however, with a round of spontaneous worker protests and factory occupations. Faced with a general strike, Prime Minister Léon Blum nimbly used the threat of further chaos to pressure employers into agreeing to a radical program of social reform. The so-called Matignon Agreements hammered out over the summer of 1936 gave workers major wage increases, the right to strike, a forty-hour week, and two weeks' paid holiday—injecting, in Blum's words, "a little beauty and sunshine into lives of hardship." The government felt sufficiently emboldened to dissolve far-right paramilitary groups and commit to national rearmament.

Yet times were probably too fraught for a left-wing government with a radical agenda to succeed. The scale of the reforms mobilized right-wing parties against the Popular Front, forcing it to dissolve in 1938. A similarly successful left-wing alliance would not be seen again until the 1980s.

The Great Pavilion Face-Off

Before his government fell apart the following year, Blum presided over a scaled-down international exposition in Paris in 1937. Though some of the glamour of the great world fairs of the nineteenth century lingered, the overall mood was altogether more somber, Picasso's epic war painting "Guernica" was on show in the pavilion of the Spanish Republic, now fighting for its life against Fascist aggression. Across the Place du Chaillot, at the heart of the exposition and in the shadow of the Eiffel Tower, the

EXPOSITION INTERNATIONALE
PARIS 1937

German and Soviet pavilions confronted each other, the former bedecked with a huge statue of a German eagle, the latter crowned with a sculpture of strident workers brandishing a hammer and sickle. It was a sinister intimation of the conflict to come.

Successive governments went along with appeasing Hitler, but in 1939 the center-left prime minister Edouard Daladier led France into war against Germany over its invasion of Poland. If there was quiet determination in some quarters, there were troubling questions too, especially after Hitler and Stalin signed the Nazi-Soviet Pact. Would the Communists show loyalty to Paris or to Moscow? Would French far-right elites prefer Hitler to Blum in power?

The way things turned out was a shock, as unanticipated as it was stunning. In the Blitzkrieg—the lightning summer campaign of 1940—Germany knocked France out of the war. The World War I hero Marshal Pétain stepped forward from the provisional government to offer Hitler a handshake of friendship. Things moved quickly. The Third Republic was dissolved. Alsace and Lorraine were returned to Germany. France was partitioned. And Pétain set up a new anti-Republican regime at the spa town of Vichy in the Massif Central. It was a devastating twist in the Franco-German tale.

CHAPTER 6

RESETTING THE NATION

France in Europe (1940–1989)

In the wake of World War II, the newly created United Nations proclaimed a Universal Declaration of Human Rights as a "common standard of achievement for all peoples and all nations" in the quest for world peace. The 1948 declaration was made in the Palais Chaillot in Paris, across the river from the Eiffel Tower, so it seemed appropriate that the document owed a manifest debt to France's 1789 Declaration of the Rights of Man.

The tacit acknowledgement of France's pioneering role in the development of human rights was all the sweeter for coming on the heels of one of the most humiliating episodes in French history. The period of Nazi occupation and rule by the Vichy puppet regime was seared indelibly into national identity and memory. But the peace of 1945 finally brought an end to more than a century of antagonism between France and Germany. In the decades to come, Europe would be the terrain for collaboration rather than conflict.

The Bitter Waters of Vichy

The peace that Nazi Germany had imposed on France in 1940 was Merovingian in its severity. Alsace-Lorraine was swallowed whole and subjected to direct German military control, along with the frontier area next to Belgium. The remainder of the country was divided in two by an east-west demarcation line roughly at the level of the river Loire. In the south, Pétain established *l'État français* (the French State) with its capital at Vichy. The northern half of the country as well as the naval ports along the Atlantic seaboard were placed under German occupation.

The Vichy regime demanded absolute loyalty to Pétain, who enjoyed quasi-dictatorial powers. Strange as it may seem in retrospect, this loyalty flowed easily at first. "The Lion of Verdun," as he was known for his commanding role in in one of France's toughest victories, was widely considered a providential and charismatic leader, two Napoleons and the Clemenceau of 1917 rolled into one.

Yet Pétain's "national revolution" soon sought to roll back the advance of republican values, with the Rights of Man a prime target. The touchstone now was not "liberty, equality, and fraternity" but "work, family, and fatherland." The Third Republic had viewed the schoolroom as the cradle of civic identity, national pride, and democratic values. The Vichy regime reversed this, favoring Catholic private schools and encouraging a populist cult of the leader through Pétainist youth groups. Traditional values espoused by the regime included measures to finagle women out of the workforce and back into the home, where they could hopefully produce enough children to boost the labor force and reduce the need for immigration. Mother's Day was promoted as a Vichy festival. Abortion was made a capital crime.

Pétain presented his regime as devoted to national regeneration in a way that rose above the petty concerns of local interests, parties, and factions, while remaining free from German domination. Later he and his supporters would claim to have acted as a "shield" against Nazi excesses. Such claims stretch credulity, for the regime worked hard to be pliable to Nazi demands. It mirrored Germany in its values and pursued repressive measures toward foreign "undesirables," trade unionists, workers, Communists, women, and Jews.

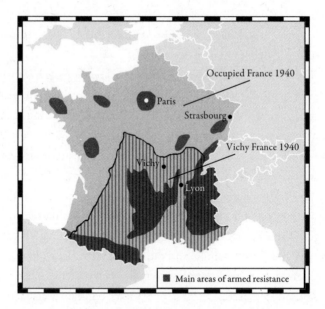

As time went on, Vichy fell ever more in line with German policies, especially after 1942 when military occupation was extended to the Vichy south. Pétain's virulently antisemitic prime minister, Pierre Laval, sought to curry favor with Hitler in the hope of incorporating France into the Nazi "New Order" in Europe. Vichy's complicity with the Final Solution included a series of police roundups of Jews. In the infamous "Vél d'Hiv" (*Vélodrome d'hiver*) incident in Paris in July 1942, some thirteen thousand Jewish inhabitants, including women and about three thousand children, were rounded up by French police and gendarmes and crammed into a cycling stadium in atrocious conditions. From there most were taken to an internment camp at Drancy on the city's outskirts before being transported in cattle cars by rail to German death camps.

Jews deemed "French" enough were spared Vél d'Hiv but would in time be lumped together with "foreign" Jews. Overall, some 75,000 Jewish people (from a population in 1940 of

330,000) would eventually be deported. They included the daughter of Alfred Dreyfus, who died in Auschwitz. Many other groups stigmatized by the Nazis such as homosexuals and Roma also followed the Drancy route. Only 2,500 of those Jews deported survived to return to France.

French policemen register foreign Jews in Pithiviers for their subsequent deportation, in May 1941.

Despite these chastening statistics, three-quarters of French Jews managed to survive the Vichy period—a relatively high rate compared with other countries under Nazi control. Yet their survival owed little or nothing to the Pétain government. The solidarity and resilience of the Jewish community were crucial factors, though help from non-Jews also counted for much. After the war, a particularly high number of individuals in France were honored as *Les Justes parmi les Nations* (the "Righteous among Nations"), for their help to Jews in distress. Popular indignation at Vichy's stigmatization of Jewish people, including the policy after 1942 of making them wear the yellow star, rebounded badly against the regime, encouraging a spirit of resistance.

This resistance gathered strength as the war continued. Initially, following the 1940 rout, many citizens of a defeated and demoralized France accepted Pétain's paternalism and the degree of cooperation with the Germans that went with it. Very few heard de Gaulle's famous BBC radio speech in June 1940 calling for an uprising, and most of those who did discounted it. Yet criticism and opposition mounted as the Vichy regime grew closer to Berlin—and as it became likely that Germany might well lose the war.

The Soviet Union's dramatic switch from Germany to the Allies in 1941 provided an important morale boost. Communist militants joined the internal resistance in droves. Leafleting of propaganda, strikes, sabotage, espionage, and targeted assassinations became more frequent. By 1944, there were as many as 260 underground networks at work, with maybe 150,000 individuals—around 2 or 3 percent of the population—committed full-time to resistance activities. Growing dislike of Vichy rapidly hardened into generalized detestation.

The brutal response to acts of resistance by both Vichy and the Nazis—including taking hostages and civilian reprisals—further diminished the regime's popularity. The *Milice*, a vicious paramilitary internal security force created in 1943 that worked hand in glove with the Gestapo, proved ironically to be an effective recruiting agent for the resistance.

There was a growing realization, too, that Germany was simply using the Vichy regime as a subterfuge to systematically pillage the French economy. This included public takeovers ("Aryanizations") of Jewish businesses and property and the wholesale plunder of artworks, but this was only the tip of the iceberg. By

1943, Germany was skimming off some 40 percent of the country's industrial production and 15 percent of its agricultural produce, while also draining France of manpower for its own industries. A million and a half French men—prisoners of war as well as labor conscripts—went on to work in Germany during the war. The work enlistment scheme, the STO (*Service du travail obligatoire*–"Compulsory Labor Service"), was introduced in 1942, though it turned out to be an act of German self-harm, for a great many young men deserted and took refuge in the *maquis*.

The Maquis

In 1942, when the German authorities brought in labor conscription, the underground resistance newspaper *Libération* carried the headline: *La jeunesse répond: merde!* Thousands of STO-dodgers "took to the *maquis*," as the saying went, heading to remote scrubland, woods and mountains to form clandestine guerrilla groups. From these hideouts, often with the help of nearby villages, the *maquisards* carried out raids and attacks on

Maquis in Châteauneuf-de-Bordette in southeast France, 1944

German targets and prepared for the Allied landings. The "Maquis" became an integral and dynamic part of the *Forces Françaises de l'Interieur* (FFI), the internal resistance.

Resistance networks were divided by geography but also by their politics, notably between Communist and Gaullist cells. From 1943, operating out of London, de Gaulle's external resistance forces, the Free French, or FFL (*Forces Françaises Libres*), acted to coordinate resistance efforts between these scattered and internally fractious groups. The left-wing bureaucrat Jean Moulin was parachuted—literally—into France in 1942 as de Gaulle's personal emissary to oversee this effort. Though Moulin was captured, tortured, and killed by the Nazis in Lyon in 1943, his work laid the foundations of the National Council of Resistance, which unified the internal networks under de Gaulle's leadership.

From the time of his radio call to arms, de Gaulle had been building an impressive resistance force outside France. This would have been unimaginable without the French colonial empire. The Franco-German agreement of 1940 had left overseas territories in Vichy's hands, but many colonies offered their support to de Gaulle from as early as autumn 1940. He quickly grasped the importance of having a territorial base from which to operate, seizing on support from French Equatorial Africa to make the Congolese city of Brazzaville the capital of "Free France." French North Africa became a battlefront for Allied forces against the Germans and Italians from 1942. By 1943, all former colonies except Indochina (which had stayed loyal to Vichy and then fallen to the Japanese) were in de Gaulle's camp.

Colonies meant men as well as territory. Around six hundred thousand colonial troops had been mobilized in 1939–1940.

Many ended up as prisoners of war in France or Germany until 1944. Some escaped to join the Free French or helped to replenish French fighting divisions. By 1944, army strength was three hundred thousand, with colonial (especially North African) troops the majority in most divisions. These played a prominent role in 1944 in the Allied landings on the Côte d'Azur in the south and, following the June D-Day landings, in operations in Normandy and northwestern France.

The (White) Liberation of Paris

De Gaulle insisted that French units should take the leading role in the liberation of Paris from German forces in August 1944. Although US and British high command agreed to this, they insisted that colonial troops be excluded from the liberating forces. This "whitening" of the city's liberation gave Parisians—and through news film the wider world—a misleading impression of the ethnically diverse forces involved in France's overall liberation.

General de Gaulle and his entourage stroll down the Champs Élysées following the liberation of Paris on August 26, 1944.

The role of the resistance in the war's endgame was important symbolically as well as militarily. Though the French could only play a supporting role to the Allies, they participated powerfully in their country's liberation, both in army formations and internal resistance operations. Probably the most significant event in national memory was the uprising in Paris in August 1944, in which the arrival of French and Allied tanks helped win the day.

Reaching the capital within hours of that victory, de Gaulle paid public tribute to the role of the Allies from the balcony of Paris's city hall, the Hôtel de Ville. He continued:

> Paris! Paris outraged! Paris broken! Paris martyred!
> But Paris liberated! Liberated by itself, liberated by
> its people with the help of the French armies, with
> the support and the help of all France, of the France
> that fights, of the only France, of the real France, of
> the eternal France!

These electrifying words, with their rapturously Francocentric spin, would echo powerfully across the years that followed. They signified that national honor had been restored. France was itself again.

Postwar Problems

The most unexpected postwar change for France would prove to be the loss of its colonies. In 1945, the French empire still covered an area slightly shy of 10 percent of the world's surface. By 1970, it was less than 1 percent.

French politicians had no inkling of what was to come. On the contrary, most anticipated the empire continuing indefinitely. De Gaulle, who enjoyed quasi-dictatorial powers until 1946 as head of the provisional postwar government, saw the empire's role as a key provider of workers, troops, and raw materials and as a market for French products. At the Brazzaville conference in 1944 he embraced France's civilizing mission for the foreseeable future. Although accepting the need for reform, he flatly ruled out a move toward autonomy. When calls for independence were heard in the aftermath of victory, notably in Algeria, Madagascar, and Indochina, de Gaulle's provisional government instructed colonial authorities not to budge. Demonstrations were suppressed with surprising brutality.

France's international stock had plummeted during the war. De Gaulle was only informed about D-Day two days in advance, nor was he invited to the Yalta and Potsdam conferences of 1945 at which the United States and Soviet Union redrew the map of Europe with Britain looking on. Even though France took an ex officio place on the UN Security Council in 1945, there was a nagging feeling that it was no longer at the top table of world affairs. The Hiroshima and Nagasaki bombs were reminders of American superpower status. All this made de Gaulle cling more tenaciously to the view that the colonies had a role to play in restoring France's place in the world.

Pétain during his trial, July 1945

Before restoring its colonial fortunes, it was first necessary to stabilize the country internally. In particular, the new authorities had to keep a lid on post-Vichy passions for revenge. The number of summary executions may have reached as many as ten thousand, while there were numerous cases of women whose heads were shaved for "horizontal collaboration." Around one hundred thousand individuals were taken into protective custody. National tribunals were established for collaborators but official executions were rare. While Laval went before the firing squad, Pétain's death sentence was commuted to life imprisonment. Most sentences involved a relatively short period of exclusion from civic life. There were partial amnesties in 1947, 1951, and 1953. Much of Vichy's state bureaucracy, in fact, remained in place.

The provisional government certainly had its hands full. French war casualties of around three hundred thousand bore no comparison with World War I, but the economy was in an almighty mess. The wounds of war ran deep. Only around half of the rail network was functioning. Despite careful rationing, inflation and food shortages were rife, while malnutrition left a durable mark on individual height and weight, especially among children. Housing stock was down 20 percent to 1939 levels. Economic bullying by the Nazis combined with war damage—some caused by Allied bombing raids—had reduced many urban areas to rubble.

D-Day's Heavy Price

The liberation of France in 1944 was no picnic. The Allies faced robust German resistance after the D-Day invasion. Strategic targeting of German army positions and port and railway facilities throughout Normandy was accompanied by more indiscriminate carpet bombing. Some eighteen thousand French civilians were killed in these British and American raids. Material damage was extreme: around three-quarters or more of housing was destroyed by Allied bombs in Caen, Le Havre, Lisieux, and Saint-Lô. This aspect of the Normandy campaign was tidied out of sight: only much later did survivors come forward to highlight a hidden cost in the price of liberation.

A French woman and a British soldier in liberated Caen, July 10, 1944

The Communist Party or PCF (*Parti communiste français*) had been the Gaullists' main resistance partner in the final Vichy years. It toyed with the idea of pushing for a transformative social revolution, with trade unions encouraging industrial militancy to raise living standards. On reflection, reconstruction seemed the higher priority, so the Communists joined the provisional government. The Gaullists and many employers met them halfway, accepting that the state had to take a more active role in society and the economy than in the 1930s. A wave of nationalizations followed, as did generous new policies regarding social security and family allowances in the spirit of a welfare state.

Victory in 1919 had not been accompanied by a feeling that the prewar political system needed radical change. But 1945 was very different. No one wanted a return to the divisiveness, corruption, and lassitude of the 1930s. While de Gaulle nurtured the myth that Vichy's "French State" was "null and void"—an illicit, imposter regime—he did not want the old one restored. Yet his personal pomp concerned his peers that changing one "providential" leader (Pétain) for another would put French democracy at risk.

A constitutional squabble over the role and powers of the executive ensued. Frustrated, de Gaulle resigned from government in 1946. He briefly returned to politics the following year, by which time a constitution had been ratified. In the event, it was not so very different from the old one: it allowed for a president with heavily restricted powers and a legislature that, with French voting patterns as they were, almost guaranteed ministerial instability. There would be more prime ministers than calendar years in the decade that followed.

This was not a good place from which to develop a strategic vision for France, for de Gaulle or indeed any party. The Communists left the government in 1947, though the PCF remained France's main working-class party and continued to trade off its wartime reputation. The onset of the Cold War meant that a Soviet-allied party was never fully acceptable in power. The PCF remained a constantly carping voice in foreign policy matters, especially after France, a co-founder of NATO in 1947, threw its support behind the United States. The country seemed squashed between two superpowers, even as it faced the defining problem of the postwar era: decolonization.

Losing an Empire

Reforms in 1946 sought to do away with the name if not the spirit of empire. Colonies were now members of a "French Union" with elected representatives and a degree of self-government. The old Caribbean island colonies were organized as departments on the French (and Algerian) model, while the most abject controls on indigenous populations were removed, forced labor was prohibited, and substantial efforts were made to boost industrial investment. A powerful colonial lobby in Paris representing self-serving settler elites kept colonies on the national agenda.

European powers tried different ways of handling the seismic decolonizing shift. Among them, France proved anything but a shining example. Its strong attachment to empire made the prospect painful and fraught with violence. Any well-intentioned reforms were made to look *dépassé* by growing calls for independence. In a way, France was a victim of its own planning. The new Universal Declaration of Human Rights, which the French example had inspired, gave populations of colonial states "the right to have rights," in the words of the German American philosopher Hannah Arendt.

An early casualty of French reformism was Indochina, where the local popularity of the pro-Communist leader Ho Chi Minh caused friction and then conflict. French generals obsessed with the 1940 humiliation at home were determined to face down military insurgency abroad. But they ended up suffering a humbling defeat at the battle of Dien Bien Phu in 1954 at the hands of Ho's military strategist Giap. The French staged a withdrawal from the region, handing the colonial baton to the United States, against whose forces Ho and Giap went on to enjoy further successes in the 1960s.

Viet Minh troops plant their flag over the captured French
headquarters at Dien Bien Phu, 1954.

Dien Bien Phu was the first major victory in modern world
history in which a colonized nation had defeated the army of its
coloniser. As such, it was an inspiration to independence movements everywhere, and nowhere more so than in Algeria. Muslim
intellectuals such as Ferhat Abbas and Messali Hadj had been
calling for independence since the late 1930s. They were now radicalized by their wartime experiences and the violent response of the
authorities to anti-French protests. In 1954, the pro-independence
FLN (*Front de libération nationale*) declared insurrection, triggering the Algerian war of independence. This would be a "dirty war,"
characterized by atrocities on both sides and the routine use of
torture by French military forces against rebels.

The Algerian conflict proved too fraught for the Fourth Republic to handle. Revolving-door ministries failed to develop a coher-
ent line and a large and intransigent white settler community did
little to help. Algerian rebels skillfully took their struggle into the
global arena, pleading their cause in the UN and at international
conferences. Intellectuals in France responded, revolted by the use

of torture by the French state and behavior that recalled the excesses of the Gestapo and the *Milice*, Vichy's hated security force. With the settler community in North Africa fearing a French sellout, the crisis reached a boil with a dramatic military-backed settler coup d'état in Algiers in May 1958. Fearing for its safety, the French government in Paris decided it could only resolve the situation by dissolving itself. A new, Fifth Republic was established and de Gaulle reinstated as president with sweeping powers.

As it turned out, de Gaulle ended the war by turning his back on the settler community and opening negotiations with the FLN. For a while, this course of action intensified the bitterness of military operations. Violence spread to metropolitan France. A number of assassination attempts targeted the new head of state, while demonstrators against the war received brutal treatment from the police in Paris in 1961. The death of Communist protesters at the Rue de Charonne subway station in Paris triggered widespread public outrage, though a massacre of Algerian protesters by police on October 17, 1961, passed relatively unnoticed at the time. The full facts would only emerge half a century later, as we shall see.

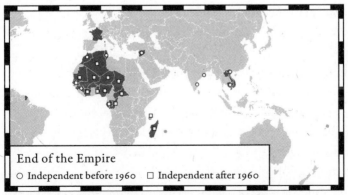

End of the Empire
○ Independent before 1960   □ Independent after 1960

Decolonization in the wake of the Algerian conflict was very rapid.

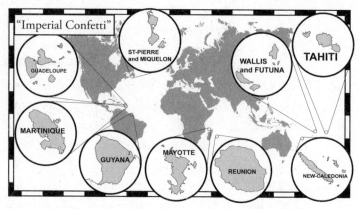

France's continuing overseas presence is small but global.

De Gaulle presented the Évian agreements of 1962 declaring an independent Algeria as a French victory. It was anything but. The war had effected regime change in Paris and caused significant loss of life. France's international prestige had taken another battering. But perhaps the biggest victim of the Algerian War was the very idea of colonialism. The loss of France's largest and most economically powerful colony knocked the stuffing out of any enthusiasm left for empire.

In any event, by 1962 there was little empire left. Many French colonies had been quietly inching toward independence long before the Algerian War: the old enclaves on the Indian subcontinent as early as 1950, Morocco and Tunisia in 1956 and Madagascar in 1958. In 1960, de Gaulle decided to grant independence to territories in sub-Saharan Africa. Within a year, all had achieved it. A once-great empire was reduced to little more than "imperial confetti."

The lack of a firm and consistent line on foreign policy had been the undoing of the Fourth Republic. By contrast, de Gaulle's authoritarian presidential style included clearly articulating the strategic goals of the Fifth. This was grounded in a desire to establish French *grandeur* on the global stage. "France without grandeur," he stated, "is not France." After Algerian independence, he navigated with added zeal between the two superpowers of the United States and Soviet Union. France needed space to make an independent mark on the world, empire or no.

The European Context

Close alliance with West Germany secured economic as well as political and diplomatic capital. European allies replaced the colonies as France's key trading partners, with France emerging for a time as the continent's most dynamic economy. Fearing destabilization of the European community, de Gaulle ensured the UK's bid to join was rejected in 1963 and 1967. Proclaiming "*Vive le Québec libre*" in Montreal on a Canadian visit ruffled British feathers too.

Though firmly in the US rather than the Soviet camp, de Gaulle withdrew from the NATO alliance to develop France's own nuclear arsenal following tests in the Algerian Sahara in 1960. The Évian agreements and the granting of autonomy to most colonies in the early 1960s allowed France to paint itself as an advocate of decolonization on the basis of human rights and self-determination. De Gaulle did not shy away from criticising the US role in Vietnam and also kept Israel at arm's length, developing close relations with newly decolonized Arab states.

Many of the leaders of newly independent states enjoyed close cultural and political links to France. The first president of Senegal, the poet Léopold Senghor, was a notable example. He and Félix Houphouet-Boigny, president of the Ivory Coast, had served in the French national assembly and had held ministerial positions. Senghor's ally in the *Négritude* movement, the poet

Aimé Césaire, was the foremost politician in Martinique during the Fifth Republic. All three backed the francophone movement, which under the auspices of the *Organisation Internationale de la Francophonie* addressed French-speakers across the globe. The French colonial empire had gone, but French was still a world language.

France's championing of the developing world was not always as altruistic as it seemed. With the exception of Guinea, its African ex-colonies agreed to retain French military forces after independence, an approach approved by the United States as a Cold War precaution. Privileged trading arrangements were also agreed on between the two sides, with France using handouts to former colonial leaders (under cover if necessary) to keep them sweet, and pro-French. The term *Françafrique* was coined to designate and denigrate these relationships as a form of neo-colonialism, underpinned by secrecy and corruption.

Trente Glorieuses

In 1968, the Paris correspondent of the London-based *Times*, John Ardagh, published a Penguin paperback titled *The New French Revolution*. Set against the somber background of France's loss of empire, his analysis revealed to English-speaking readers the striking transformation of French society, culture, and the economy that he had witnessed since the 1940s. His argument was underscored a few years later by the French sociologist Jean Fourastié, who coined the term *Trente Glorieuses* ("Thirty Glorious Years") to describe the years from 1945 to 1975. An annual growth rate of more than 5 percent made it the period of fastest economic expansion in French history.

The *Trente Glorieuses* did not feel very glorious at the time, at least not at first. In a graphic expression of hard-felt social

A fashion model has her Dior dress torn from her back after being pelted with eggs in public, October 1947.

inequalities, working-class women in Montmartre in 1948 tore the Christian Dior "New Look" dress off the back of a fashion model: they resented the luxuriant use of expensive cloth in the dress's full skirt that seemed to rub salt into the wounds of postwar hardship. All the same, Ardagh and Fourastié were correct in highlighting the vastness of the social changes under way. Both writers also put their finger on a feature of this achievement that was particular to France, namely, the use of central planning mechanisms to reshape the economy. These rekindled a French fondness for *dirigisme* that stretched back to the seventeenth century.

A General Planning Commission was created in 1946 under the Gaullist *résistant* Jean Monnet to superintend economic recovery and modernization by setting five-year targets for growth. The first phase of *le Plan Monnet*, as it became familiarly known, prioritized infrastructure and production from 1947 to 1951, a sensible move given the extent of war damage. The second phase shifted the focus onto consumption and housing. Research institutions were set up to provide accurate data on economic trends, smoothing the commission's way. Generous levels of US investment were channeled through the Marshall Aid Plan in ways that buttressed the plan's objectives. There was a strong sense of the state being responsible for material improvement to people's lives.

The Making of the EU

The creation in 1951 of the European Coal and Steel Community (ECSC) was the most eye-catching achievement in the first phase of Monnet's plan. Although Italy and the Benelux countries (Belgium, the Netherlands, Luxembourg) were also signatories, Germany was France's key partner. This was only the beginning of closer links with Europe. In 1956, the group went on to ratify the Treaty of Rome, which created the European Economic Community (EEC: better known in English as the Common Market). In subsequent decades, the group expanded its members, with Denmark, Ireland, and the UK entering in 1973 and Greece in 1981. Trade, agriculture, and industry were progressively integrated across

member states. The EEC, subsumed into the European Union (EU) in 1993, became one of the largest and most powerful economic units in the world. France had lost an empire but regained its place at the heart of Europe.

Baby Boom

Another distinctive feature of the *Trente Glorieuses* was France's remarkable demographic transformation. As the first industrializing country to adopt contraception on a systematic basis, France's low birth rate since the nineteenth century had caused its population growth to lag well behind its neighbors. After 1945, thanks largely to improved welfare provisions, the birth rate soared. At the end of the war, the population had stood at forty million. By 1970, it was fifty million, a rise of a quarter in a quarter of a century. Growth continued, though less dramatically, to just shy of sixty million in 2000 and around sixty-six million today in mainland France.

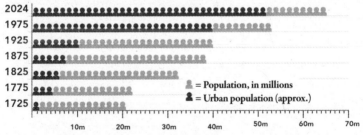

The decline of rural France became notable from the last half of the twentieth century.

The unparalleled postwar baby boom strongly influenced social attitudes, especially when these boomers entered adolescence. By the 1970s, at least one French person in three was under twenty years old. Population growth also triggered an expansion of demand within the economy while helping to increase the labor force needed to feed it.

Even so, the speed of economic growth after 1945 required foreign workers to fill the gap. Most newcomers came as before from Spain, Italy, Belgium, and Portugal—but from the 1950s, North Africans started appearing in greater numbers. There had been 20,000 Algerians in France in 1945. In 1970, there were 210,000. Total immigration numbers rose over the same period, from 1.7 million to 4 million, along with a million or more white settlers, known as *pieds noirs*, who had resettled in France after the Évian agreements.

Most immigrants entered the economy in menial or manual trades. They also settled overwhelmingly in towns and cities, spurring the rapid urbanization of the period. France had been one of the most rural of the leading industrialized states until World War II. It was only in the 1930s that the inhabitants of towns began to outnumber country-dwellers for the first time; the tipping point for England had been a century earlier, in 1830. The urban share of France's population continued to grow to 60 percent by 1960 and carried on rising—to over 80 percent today. These figures also reflect a sizeable rural exodus linked to Monnet-backed plans to mechanize farming.

Foreign and internal migration, coupled with rising life expectancy, created a need for accommodation that overwhelmed French cities. Housing stock had still not recovered from war damage and private building was not prioritized in the first iteration of the Monnet plan. Shantytowns sprang up on the outskirts and in the suburbs of major cities. Paris was a major draw: there were nearly a hundred of these *bidonvilles* in its immediate vicinity by the 1960s. But in the late 1950s governments began to invest more heavily in *grands ensembles* (housing projects) of lower-income housing, known as HLMs (*habitations à loyer modéré*). Extensive, high-rise projects became a feature of the suburbs of French cities—and soon became a source of social unrest.

Saint-Denis *bidonville*, with newly built housing in the background

French Flair

Despite this darker underbelly, the *Trente Glorieuses* saw France recover its cultural éclat on the world stage. If Christian Dior's dresses, with their curvaceous line, cinched waist, and luxuriant folds, stirred resentment in some quarters, there was no denying their international appeal. They made France seem chic again— elegant, fashionable, and enviable. Dior's New Look was popularized by *Life* and other US magazines, which also swooned over emerging *haute couture* talents such as Hubert de Givenchy, Pierre Balmain, and, from the 1960s, the prodigious Yves Saint-Laurent. "It's so French!" was an admiring mantra heard around the world. Coco Chanel had already given the world the little black dress and Chanel No. 5 perfume. Sales for the latter perked up when Marilyn Monroe disclosed in an interview with *Life* in 1952 that she went to bed wearing nothing else.

Infatuation with "New France" went much further than fashion. No fewer than six francophone writers were awarded the

Nobel prize for literature in the quarter-century after 1945: André Gide (1947), François Mauriac (1952), Albert Camus (1957), the poet Saint-John Perse (1960), Jean-Paul Sartre (1964), and the Irishman Samuel Beckett (1969). Sartre (who rejected the prize) was perhaps the most famous of them all—his existentialist philosophy, with its blend of activism and pessimism, proving to have global appeal.

The postwar period was a golden age for French cinema too. Marcel Carné's *Les Enfants du Paradis* (1945) gained legendary status, while from the 1950s the *Nouvelle Vague* (New Wave) of directors such as François Truffaut, Jean-Luc Godard, Eric Rohmer, Agnès Varda, and Claude Chabrol reimagined cinema. The directors acknowledged huge debts to American filmmakers. Hollywood paid France back handsomely in kind: great musicals such as *An American in Paris* (1951), *Moulin Rouge* (1953), and *Can-Can* (1960) presented Paris back to itself tinsel-wrapped. Imitation was the sincerest form of flattery.

The post-1945 Parisian mood was strikingly captured by the school of humanist photographers, including Henri Cartier-Bresson, Willie Ronis, Brassai, and André Kertesz, and in particular Robert Doisneau. His famous *The Kiss by the Hôtel de Ville* published in 1950 in *Life*, was to become the most popular fridge magnet of all time.

French flair also galvanized science and engineering. France gained a reputation for innovation in cutting-edge nuclear and hydroelectric power projects. The national rail service underwent modernization, with high-speed trains (TGVs: *trains à grande vitesse*) setting new service standards and establishing world-record speeds of well over two hundred miles per hour. The Anglo-French Concorde made its maiden flight in 1969. On that flight, it was said that the food served to guests marked the first use of the term *nouvelle cuisine,* which was lighter, fresher, and more elegantly presented than the classic bourgeois and peasant dishes for which France was already famous. Nouvelle cuisine was just the first in a long line of dietary fads in which France would lead the world.

Doisneau's Kiss

Was this so-spontaneous kiss in fact staged? An ongoing legal dispute over copyright kept the image in the headlines, but in 2005 the case was settled when Françoise Bornet came forward with a copy of the photograph that Doisneau gave her when, as a twenty-year-old drama student, he had asked her and her boyfriend to pose. Bornet died in 2023, 150,000 euros richer from having recently auctioned the photograph.

Consumer Plenty

These home-grown cultural products were not just for export. One of the striking features of the economy from the late 1950s was the rise of a consumer culture that put elite commodities within popular reach. The steady and consistent rise in wages helped, but it was also a question of taste and convenience. A good deal of rhetoric was spent attacking the "Coca-Colonization" of the French economy, but in practice, US investment in industry boosted the economy, US imports helped stock the shelves, and the globalization of French style owed much to US media.

Cars, refrigerators, washing machines, and televisions all became affordable objects for the working classes. In the cultural sphere, the cheap paperback—or *livre de poche*—put literary classics within reach of all from the early 1950s. On the back of Dior's New Look, *prêt-à-porter* clothes brought high fashion to working-class women. The extension of paid holidays for workers—from two weeks to three (1969), then four (1982), and eventually five (1992)—provided more time for the leisure and cultural consumption that were key features of the "New France" created since the war.

The Authentic Taste of France

The idea of authenticating foods from certain places dates back to 1411, when the French king gave this privilege to the producers of Roquefort cheese, in the village of the same name. But the modern history of the quality control system known as AOC (*appellation d'origine contrôlée*) really starts in the 1930s, with efforts to guarantee the quality of wines from the great growing areas of Burgundy, the Bordelais, and Champagne. Its use extended to spirits (Cognac, Armagnac, Calvados), cheeses (Roquefort, Brie, Camembert, Comté), lentils (Le Puy), honey (Corsica), and even chickens (Bresse). Many of these achieved global brand status, and the list continues to grow. When the AOC system works well, it protects the interests of consumers and producers alike.

May '68

The month of May 1968 saw the biggest wave of industrial action since the days of the Popular Front in the 1930s. Numerous factories were occupied and a general strike was called. As many as ten million workers withheld their labor, making it the biggest strike in French history.

It was soon clear that this amounted to much more than an industrial action. Working-class strikers had latched on to a movement that began in the university dormitories of the postwar baby boomers. The student revolt that kickstarted the so-called May Events began as a protest against a ban on cohabitation on the Paris Nanterre University campus. After a heavy-handed response by university authorities, students took to the streets—at first in Paris but then in provincial university cities—where they were met by police tear-gas canisters, beatings, and baton charges. With television reports fanning the flames, the protests then spread like wildfire to target the broader regime. Within days a small blaze in Nanterre threatened to consume the Fifth Republic.

The events of May 1968 proved to be less about old-style working-class militancy than about a perceived need across French society for wholesale change, including demands for new and more satisfying ways of living. Workplace, family, public institutions— no structure of power was beyond reproach. Traditional labor strikes were complemented by an array of other forms of protest, from direct action, occupations, demonstrations, and crowd mobilizations to improvised posters and graffiti. The status quo seemed to totter. At the height of the crisis, de Gaulle actually took flight from France (as it was later discovered, to ensure the loyalty of French troops stationed in Germany in case there was a total breakdown of order). As the graffiti of that summer proclaimed, *L'imagination au pouvoir!* the imagination seemed to be on the brink of power.

Global Counterculture

The May Events in France tapped into a global political current that thrilled the baby-boomer generation, born after 1945. Its main points of reference were the Vietnam War, the Cultural Revolution in China, the US Civil Rights Movement, opposition to South African apartheid, and Czech protests against Soviet hegemony in

The courtyard of the Sorbonne University is occupied by students in May 1968 in Paris.

Eastern Europe. A counterculture transcending the lefts, rights, and other certainties of mainstream politics was emerging based around opposition to war, colonialism, racism, social inequality, mass consumerism, and materialism—though its adherents danced to rock music and its wardrobe was blue denim.

With domestic and international TV crews on full alert and channels giving running reportage on the "May Events," the whole world watched and in some cases took inspiration. Student radicals like Danny "the Red" Cohn-Bendit became media celebrities. After decades in which France's venerable tradition of revolt had been consigned to history, 1968 made it seem that revolution was relevant again, even chic.

Ironically, the Fifth Republic had been doing rather well before the May events rudely set it rocking on its foundations. Both de Gaulle's accession to power and his decision to grant Algerian independence had been accepted by the vast majority of the French population, as had France's participation in Europe and de Gaulle's quest for an independent foreign policy. All this put the Fifth Republic in good stead, especially as the material gains of the *Trente Glorieuses* continued to accrue, with employment high and prices stable.

France's expansive foreign policy in the 1960s had not, however, been mirrored in domestic affairs. Though de Gaulle pushed a social agenda and buttressed the nation's welfare system, he rarely seemed to listen to new voices bubbling up from beneath. Despite the rise of popular consumerism, social inequality did not lessen and indeed seemed to have gotten worse. State censorship was heavy and cumbersome. The government's control over TV and radio channels gave a sense that it wanted citizens to hear only the official version. The green light given to police violence in strikes and demonstrations fed this suspicion.

Divide to Rule

The multifaceted nature of the 1968 protests made them all the more formidable, but this may have helped the regime to survive. Ignoring the students, Prime Minister Georges Pompidou took the trade unions to one side and negotiated the Grenelle Accords, which echoed the Popular Front's 1936 Matignon Agreements. Offering massive wage increases and a host of improvements to work conditions, the terms were generous enough to get workers off the streets and back on the job. Peeling away the unions drained some of the effervescence from the student-led protests. Having played his cards adroitly, and with the protests on the brink of fizzling out, de Gaulle's master stroke was to call a snap election as he was able under the provisions of the constitution. France's silent majority turned out at the polls to produce the biggest right-wing victory in the history of the republic.

In purely political terms, the May Events were not at all a turning point for France. But they were a pivot around which France's sense of itself changed, especially in the cultural sphere. The episode and its aftermath also changed the French public mood and transformed its horizon of expectations. But the upheaval was certainly too much for de Gaulle himself. He had grown old in a France more full of young people than ever before. In 1969, he resigned and retired completely from public life, dying two years later. The providential figure who had turned up for three rendezvous with history—in 1940, 1944, and 1958—had this time missed the bus. He left as presidential successor his prime minister, Georges Pompidou.

Although government had inveigled itself out of the crisis by buying off the unions, this form of collective bargaining was beginning to lose its edge. Trade union membership was in decline and from the 1980s would be in freefall. In 1968, the Communist trade union, the CGT, had backed the government rather than the student rebels, whom they viewed as spoiled bourgeois brats. Their accommodation by the Gaullist regime left vacant a political space on the left that was occupied by a motley range of *gauchistes*, that is, left-leaning *-istes* of various persuasions (Trotskyists, Maoists, anarchists, and so on), often organized in tiny yet vehement *groupuscules*. New forms of activism emerged post-1968 that bypassed traditional trade unions.

Political activists on the left began to operate in ways we now associate with social movements. The first step was to incorporate the panoply of militant maneuvers on show in the May Events, from demonstrations to provocations and graffiti. The second was to look to veteran *soixante-huitards* ("Sixty-Eighters") for leadership. Third, campaigns would focus on single or closely connected issues, many drawing inspiration from related movements outside French borders. An early emphasis on the treatment of immigrant workers, for example, sparked a lively anti-racist movement to which intellectual icons such as Jean-Paul Sartre and Michel Foucault contributed. This campaign had mixed results, with a law in 1972 banning hate speech but another in 1974 formally ending open immigration.

Personal Freedoms

Despite generalized distaste for American foreign policy, US-style political agitation played a significant part in French social movements. American "Second Wave" activists galvanized French feminists, for example. Surprisingly for a country that gave the world one of modern feminism's foundational texts—Simone de Beauvoir's *The Second Sex* (1949)–the feminist movement developed slowly in France. Women were only given the vote in 1944 and still played a limited role in political life. The patriarchal spirit of the Napoleonic Code still hung over women's claims to legal, financial, and sexual autonomy.

The May Events were an important milestone but hardly a revolution for women. The rank sexism of many *gauchistes* suggested that there had to be another way. The *Mouvement de libération des femmes* (MLF) was founded on the US model in 1970 on a Parisian university campus. The following year, de Beauvoir penned its so-called Manifesto of the 343—more than three hundred women in public life who stated they had had an abortion, at the time still an illegal act. The feminist push for more liberal policies over sexuality built up a head of steam under the centrist politician Valéry Giscard d'Estaing, elected president of the Republic in 1974 following the sudden death of Pompidou. Giscard passed laws that legalized and facilitated the sale of contraceptives. His government generally combatted the outworn patriarchalism of the Napoleonic Civil Code.

More substantial gains for women would have to wait, often for several more decades. Much the same was true for the gay community. As with the MLF, gay activists and lesbian feminists drew inspiration from the United States and specifically the 1969 Stonewall riots in New York. The *Front Homosexuel d'Action Révolutionnaire* (Homosexual Front for Revolutionary Action), created in 1971, mirrored the American Gay Liberation Front, albeit militating in the spirit of May '68. It soon burned itself out, though the age

The French writer, existentialist philosopher, political activist, and feminist
Simone de Beauvoir during the Bobigny abortion trial in 1972

of consent for homosexual acts was reduced from 21 to 18
in 1974 and then to 15 in 1982 (which brought it to the level
established for heterosexuals in 1945).

The mood of greater personal and social freedom was confirmed
by the election of François Mitterrand, a Socialist, as president in
1981. A veteran of the wheeling-and-dealing Fourth Republic who
had twice failed to secure the presidency, Mitterrand clawed a way
back for the parliamentary left from its electoral nadir in 1968. He
did this first by tapping into the spirit of May '68, notably through his
ally Michel Rocard, who had swum up through *groupuscule* culture.
Secondly, he cleverly combined forces with the Communist PCF in a
"Common Program" that attracted broad electoral support. Though
both parties subsequently went cool on the arrangement, there was

enough remaining goodwill across the left to get Mitterrand over the line as president.

Mitterrand's success in 1981 marked the left's first return to power since the Popular Front in 1936. Like that precedent, it created a great wave of hope for radical change, all the more so as the Fifth Republic placed so much power in presidential hands. Some eye-catching reforms followed: a string of nationalizations, abolition of the death penalty, acceptance of greater freedom for radio and TV broadcasting, a thirty-five-hour week, and generous social welfare reforms. The money needed to fund the program would come, Mitterrand assured the public, from economic growth.

That was not going to happen. The *Trente Glorieuses* had run out of steam in the mid 1970s, mainly due to shifts in the global economy. The 1944 Bretton Woods currency arrangement that pegged the dollar to gold broke down in 1971, causing the dollar to devalue, which triggered severe economic turbulence around the world. Then came the decision of Middle Eastern oil producers to curb exports following the 1973 Arab-Israeli War, another massive blow to the Western economies.

Most of the industrial achievements of the *Trente Glorieuses* were powered by fossil fuels, so the 1973 embargo raised a question mark regarding France's dependence on coal and oil. A creditable run for president by the sociologist René Dumont in 1974 as the ecology candidate further raised environmental awareness. The emerging ecological movement raised strong support for peasants in the remote Larzac plateau in the Massif Central who protested throughout the 1970s against the creation of a military base there. One of Mitterrand's early acts was to withdraw the threat to Larzac, but the Socialists could not contain the environmentalist

current. A Green Party emerged in the 1980s, with veteran pro-
tester and former *soixante-huitard* Daniel ('Danny the Red')
Cohn-Bendit among its leaders. It was soon nibbling away at the
Socialist vote in local and European elections.

A similar picture emerged in regional politics. An important
law passed by the Socialists in 1982 sought to devolve many powers
to the provinces. The administrative tasks of the ninety or so
departments that had emerged since 1790 were reallocated to some
twenty-two regions (reduced in 2018 to thirteen). There were prac-
tical reasons for the law, but the changes also revitalized regional
politics. Many Corsicans saw it as a first step toward autonomy, for
example. The decentralizing tendency was also evident in a more
accepting attitude toward regional languages such as Breton and
Occitan, with a growing sense that they formed part of French cultural patrimony. In the same spirit, de Gaulle's minister of culture,
the novelist and writer André Malraux, instituted a dozen provincial *maisons de la culture* to act as cultural hubs and animators
outside the capital.

The Anglo-Saxon Model

By the time Mitterrand came to power, France was struggling to
adjust to a crisis in the international world economy. An alliance
led by President Ronald Reagan and Prime Minister Margaret
Thatcher sought a way out by implementing neo-liberal policies:
reducing taxation, cutting welfare to help balance the budget,
deregulating the market, freeing trade, and encouraging privat-
ization.

In retrospect, Mitterrand's wistful socialism looked like a
dinosaur awaiting slaughter. And so it proved. Within a year or
two he was walking back earlier promises and good intentions,

losing the support of the Communists, and increasingly falling in line with the international order. Poor polling in legislative elections in 1986 saw him forced to accept a right-wing ministry with its rising star Jacques Chirac as prime minister. "Cohabitation" tested the robustness of the Fifth Republic's constitution and confirmed Mitterrand's chameleon-like survival instinct. But it also marked France's grudging enlistment into the neoliberal world order.

The social and economic signs were depressing. Recession linked to the 1974 oil crisis signaled the end of the good old days of record-breaking economic expansion. Annual growth rates of 5 percent became a thing of the past. Levels slowed to 2 to 3 percent, sometimes less. Unemployment and inflation stalked the corridors of the Fifth Republic, joblessness rates creeping upward from postwar levels of less than 2 percent to nearly 10 percent by the mid-1980s. In the early 1990s, they passed that milestone. Inflation had bumped along at between 2 and 4 percent during the 1960s, but by the mid 1970s it was over 10 percent. It would stay at around that level through the 1980s.

Political discontent soon followed with the sudden re-entry onto the scene of the far right, in the shape of the *Front National*. Founded in 1972 by Jean-Marie Le Pen, the party made anti-immigration, racism, and antisemitism its calling cards. Initially, Le Pen failed to get enough support to stand as president in 1981, which saved him from an almost certain hiding. Yet the group came of age in the European elections of 1984 and the national legislative elections of 1986, taking about 10 percent of the vote in both. The French political landscape was on the cusp of a further transformation.

The Rise of the Far Right

No one can have imagined when Le Pen founded the National Front that it would survive more than half a century, let alone become a powerful force in French politics. A public Holocaust denier, Le Pen had emerged out of a neo-fascist milieu, and his party could have passed as a far-right *groupuscule*. The shameful record of the far right in the Vichy years seemed to have insulated the French from any attraction to such figures, while the economic success of the *Trente Glorieuses* made their policies seem anachronistic. Those days were clearly over.

Grands Projets

Against a background of economic torpor, rising discontent, and far-right extremism, Mitterrand unveiled a series of eye-catching *Grands Projets*. Many were the fruit of his predecessors' labors, notably a major cleanup of public monuments, instigated by Culture Minister Malraux in the 1960s. In Paris, an ostentatious modernist arts center was commissioned by its namesake Georges Pompidou, and the sprawling railway station on the Quai d'Orsay was converted into a museum for nineteenth-century culture, for which Giscard d'Estaing had given the green light.

By 1986, when Mitterrand opened the Musée d'Orsay, a whole raft of these Grand Projects were waiting in the pipeline. In time, Paris would be adorned by the Parc de La Villette, I. M. Pei's glass pyramid at the Louvre, the Institute of the Arab World, the national library (now the Bibliothèque François Mitterrand), a colossal monumental Arche de la Défense on the western edge of the city, and the Bastille Opéra. The opening of the new opera house on the Place de la Bastille was deliberately scheduled for

1989, to mark the bicentenary of the French Revolution that had started on that very spot. The year 1989 would be pivotal for France in this and much else besides.

The glass pyramid at the Louvre, one of several *Grands Projets* completed in 1989

CHAPTER 7

MEMORIES, PROSPECTS, UNCERTAINTIES

1989–Present

In the summer of 1989, a young American political scientist, Francis Fukuyama, published a speculative essay titled "The End of History?" He argued that the collapse of Communism would presage the global triumph of liberal capitalism. The claim rocketed its author to global fame and fortune, and gained him a reputation as a prophet when the fall of the Berlin Wall that autumn was followed by not only German unification but also the overthrow of Communist regimes across Eastern Europe and in the Soviet Union, and an end to the Cold War that had divided the world for nearly half a century.

1789 and 1989

Many Germans saw in the fall of the Berlin Wall in 1989 an echo of the fall of the Bastille in 1789, a point not lost on French President François Mitterrand. At the international summit held in Paris to celebrate the French Revolution's bicentenary, he was pressed by British Prime Minister Margaret Thatcher to admit that the English Magna Carta had been a harbinger of freedom long before the French Revolution. Though scrupulously diplomatic in his response, he pointed out that it was in 1789, and not 1215, that revolutionaries the world over had found "an ideal in whose name the people would fight."

The same year also saw a seemingly trivial newspaper story swell spectacularly into a national *cause célèbre* that kept both Bastille and Berlin off the front pages. Three young Islamic women of Moroccan descent refused to remove their headscarf (*foulard*) or hijab in their school in Creil, which was located in a Parisian *banlieue* (suburb). A bad-tempered media storm over this *affaire du foulard* foreshadowed emerging lines of tension within French society: the banlieues as a problem, the place of women within the republic, and the integration of second-generation immigrants from across the old empire. The issue also provided a platform for the far right, which sought to reattune France to the politics of blame, hate, and resentment.

Memory Wars and Memory Laws

"The facts may prove me wrong," de Gaulle once remarked to one of his ministers, "but history will prove me right." "But, *mon général*," replied the minister. "I thought that history was written with facts."

New memory wars broke out in the final years of the twentieth century, as rival interpretations of the nation's past faced off. By 1989, the French public appeared less interested in memorializing the Revolution two centuries earlier than remembering a more recent historical episode: Vichy. Since 1944, de Gaulle and others had promoted a narrative about World War II in which the French people had been fully committed to resistance against Vichy and the Nazis. In the 1970s and 1980s, however, the facts started to catch up with this *mythe résistantiel*.

Marcel Ophuls's four-hour Franco-German production *Le Chagrin et la pitié* ("The Sorrow and the Pity") first threatened to pull the rug from under the established Gaullist narrative. The film gave a portrayal of wartime Clermont-Ferrand that showed the population ruled less by Germans than by fellow Frenchmen collaborating freely with their Nazi occupiers. Shown on German television in 1971, it was deemed too incendiary for broadcast in France, though it was shown to packed houses in theaters. The American historian Robert Paxton's *Vichy France*, published the following year, further revealed how closely the Vichy government and its bureaucracy collaborated with Hitler's Germany in the deportation of Jews. Vichy's defense, that it had tried to shield the French from Nazi demands, had always seemed flimsy. Now it was revealed as an outright lie.

A series of trials of public figures from the Vichy era ensured that the issue remained in the public eye until the turn of the century. One of the most dramatic cases involved a Gestapo officer

Maurice Papon and his lawyer Jean-Marc Varaut on October 14, 1997, at Bordeaux's courthouse during his trial for wartime crimes against humanity

Klaus Barbie, the so-called Butcher of Lyon, who had tortured to death the Resistance hero Jean Moulin. Barbie was extradited from Bolivia and put on trial in 1987 for crimes against humanity, most notably the deportation and deaths of hundreds of Jews, including many children. He was sentenced to life imprisonment.

Equally dramatic was a long-running case against the patrician career bureaucrat Maurice Papon. His closeness to political elites on both left and right after 1945 had helped him to lead a seemingly charmed life. But in 1998, after long, drawn-out preliminaries and a trial, he was sentenced to ten years' imprisonment for his involvement in the deportation of Jews from the Bordeaux area where he had served under Vichy. His activities were also adjudged to be crimes against humanity.

De Gaulle and his followers had always argued that *l'Etat français* of Pétain was illegitimate and thus France could bear no responsibility for its actions. Yet the Papon case showed how far the stain of Vichy had permeated the postwar republics. This arch political insider had played a key role in other dark chapters in France's postwar history, holding high office in the Algerian administration in the 1950s when it routinely used torture against rebels. And as prefect of police in Paris in the early 1960s, Papon was also directly responsible for the police meting out deadly force against Communist and Algerian protesters.

"Here we drown Algerians"

On October 19, 1961, Algerian demonstrators detained by the police were murdered and their bodies thrown into the Seine outside the police prefecture on the Ile de la Cité in the heart of Paris. This photograph was taken shortly afterward, close to where the incidents took place. Estimates of the numbers killed still vary: it was certainly scores and perhaps hundreds. Not only did the murders take place on Papon's watch, he played an active role in the massacre and hushed it up in the press. The investigative journalism of Jean-Luc Einaudi brought the case to public attention in the 1990s. After Papon's conviction in 1998 for his Vichy past, the mayor of Paris, Bertrand Delanoë, placed a commemorative plaque on the "Algerian bridge" in 2001.

Close to the site of the deaths, this graffiti was removed by the authorities almost immediately.

In 1990, as debate raged over Papon and his ilk, the Mitterrand government passed laws against hate crimes, citing as examples antisemitism, xenophobia, and Holocaust denial. This was the first of a series of *lois mémorielles* (memory laws) that sought to bring national memory more in line with the historical record. In 1995, on the anniversary of the infamous Vél d'Hiv roundup of 1942, President Jacques Chirac formally apologized for the complicity of the French state in the treatment of Jews in World War II. In 2001, a law formally recognizing the Armenian genocide was passed, followed by another ackowledging slavery and the slave trade as crimes against humanity. Memory wars had inspired memory laws that were to haunt debates on French identity well into the twenty-first century.

European Integration

Largely unnoticed, 1989 also marked the longest period in modern French history in which the country was not at war with one of its neighbors, overtaking the forty-three years of peace between the Franco-Prussian war of 1870–1871 and World War I.

The binding of the French and German economies into a European framework had produced a significant peace dividend. The end of the Cold War and German unification further accelerated European integration. Following the accession of Spain and Portugal in 1986, the EEC contained twelve members. That number would more than double, particularly with the inclusion of former Soviet Eastern European states. It seemed there was greater prosperity as well as safety in numbers.

Stiff economic competition in this globalized, neo-liberal world encouraged further European integration. The Schengen agreement in 1985 introduced freedom of movement within the bloc as a whole, while the Maastricht Treaty of 1992 establishing the European Union agreed upon the principle of a common foreign and security policy, closer cooperation in domestic issues such as justice, and the introduction of European citizenship. A single currency, the euro, would be introduced in 2002.

Such supra-national moves caused ripples within such a traditionally nationalistic state as France. Far-right politicians seized on the idea that Europe was trampling over the French people. This Euroskepticism played a strategic role in the sound rejection in the 2005 referendum of a proposed European constitution. Even so, the troubles of the UK, which withdrew from the union after the Brexit vote in 2016, would serve as a solemn warning. As any idea of a "Frexit" became far less appetizing, the National Front turned instead to stirring up anti-immigrant feeling.

"Rather the Crook than the Fascist"

The National Front party performed well in the 1997 elections, taking 15 percent of the national vote, but it was the 2002 presidential campaign that marked its break-through moment. Jean-Marie Le Pen beat the Socialist candidate Lionel Jospin to secure a place in the runoff against the incumbent Jacques Chirac, whose financial integrity was seriously questioned. In the final round of voting, the slogan "Rather the crook than the fascist" carried the day for Chirac. Yet the fact that he wiped the floor with Le Pen in the final poll was less important than the arrival of the National Front as a serious contender in national politics.

Turn Right after the Church

"Left" and "right" originated as political terms in the French Revolution. This broad division became firmly impressed on the electoral geography of the country, with religion remaining a key indicator of political affiliation well into the twentieth century. Over four-fifths of Catholic voters in 1965 opted for de Gaulle, while three-quarters of nonbelievers chose the Socialist candidate, Mitterrand. Strongly Catholic areas—Brittany, the northeast, and the Massif Central—remained bastions of the Catholic Right, in a pattern clearly observable since the 1790s.

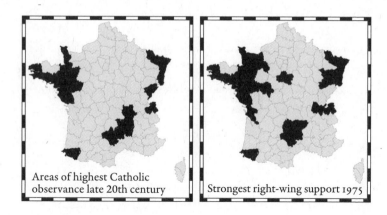

Areas of highest Catholic observance late 20th century

Strongest right-wing support 1975

By the 1970s, two centuries later, these deep and enduring correlations were beginning to break down. Growing secularisation had thinned the ranks of Catholic right-wingers, while monarchism was clearly a dead duck. The right began to view the Republic as a legitimate framework for political life. De Gaulle had played an important role in the "republicanization" of right-wing politics, showing that a strong president could be a bulwark of law and order. Even the far right—which in the war had invested strongly in Pétainism—came around to accepting the idea too, in time representing itself as more republican than the Republic.

A changing international landscape also impinged on the French electorate. The French Communist Party had traditionally been the party of choice for working-class voters and the unions, regularly attracting a large share of national votes—a quarter in the postwar years and rarely below one-fifth in the early 1960s. But the PCF lost support in the wake of 1968 and after its electoral pact with the Socialists. By contrast, the latter picked up voters from the political center ground, many of them social movements with large *soixante-huitard* contingents.

A plunge in union membership contributed to the Communists' decline. Indeed, the French rate of unionization became one of the lowest in Europe. But the last straw proved to be the overthrow of communist parties in the Soviet Union and Eastern Europe. Internal party reforms failed to stop the rot. The PCF's share of the national vote would thereafter bump along at around 5 percent. The Communists' loss was the National Front's gain.

Changes to the political map also mirrored changes in the French economy. Since the 1970s, a long-term shift of jobs to the service sector, characteristic of most western economies, steadily eroded farming and industry. Sluggish growth and the outsourcing of production overseas caused a collapse of Communist support in areas with a traditionally large working-class electorate. Mines and factories closed in coal and steel regions of the northeast, in the so-called red belt of working-class voters surrounding Paris, and in pockets of industry further south. Independent farmers and winegrowers in particular drifted away from the parties of the left toward the National Front. The presence near the Mediterranean of a large number of *pieds-noirs*—white settlers evacuated from Algeria after 1962—helped to bolster the performance of the far right in what had once been the *Midi rouge* ("Red South").

In all these areas, high levels of unemployment—which had stabilized at around 8 percent after peaking in the 1990s—also played a role in disenchanting voters with the traditional mainline parties. Ironically, economic restructuring and labor-force reductions boosted productivity. France became one of the world's top food exporters. All the same, there would be no going back to the *Trente Glorieuses*.

France in the World

For all its struggles in recent decades, France remains an elite global power. It retains its place as founder-member of the UN Security Council and has been a member of the Group of Seven (G7) nations since its inception as the G6 in 1975. France is the world's seventh-largest economy, competing with the UK for second place in Europe behind Germany. It is one of nine states known to have nuclear weapons and has rejoined NATO at an operational level.

France has been prominent among world powers in assuming a peacekeeping role in crisis areas, including Africa, the Middle East, and even Europe, following the breakup of Yugoslavia. It is a key player in many international bodies, including UNESCO, whose headquarters are in Paris. French is an official language not only of UNESCO but also of the UN, the EU, and the OECD (Organisation for Economic Cooperation and Development), among others.

France's colonial past buttresses its global reach. Often tiny and remote from France, its remaining territories still contain nearly three million people. The most significant of them are the so-called *départements et régions d'outre-mer et collectivités d'outre-mer*, known as the DROM-COM. The DROMs are largely vestiges of France's first colonial empire, notably Guadeloupe, Martinique, and French Guiana in the Caribbean, as well as Réunion in the Indian Ocean. Most considerable among the COMs are French Polynesia (including Tahiti) and New Caledonia. Living standards within them are lower than in France itself and unemployment is very high in some cases, but conditions are typically better than in neighboring states.

Remnants of Empire

Devolution overseas has been hastened by the blithely neo-colonial character of certain French initiatives. The use of parts of French Polynesia for nuclear testing between the 1960s and the 1990s has hardly endeared France to locals, for example, especially when it was learned that nuclear fallout across the region was much heavier than originally thought. From the mid-1970s, vigorous calls for independence have been voiced by the indigenous Kanak population in New Caledonia. Over the years, murky maneuvers in Africa under the banner of *Françafrique* have also fostered powerful independence movements in formerly French west and central Africa. In the early 2020s, the Pan-African argument—boosted by the sly deployment of Russian and Chinese soft power—began to be heard again in debates within formerly French parts of sub-Saharan Africa. The rise of Islamist movements across the region has also undermined France's strong position there.

A 914-kiloton Licorne (Unicorn) bomb is tested at Mururoa Atoll in French Polynesia on July 3, 1970.

La Francophonie

While metropolitan France can boast some 66 million French speakers, there are around 250 million globally. French is an official language in twenty-eight countries. Six or seven of these are independent states in Europe, but the biggest battalions are found in former French and Belgian colonies in Africa and in Haiti, which recognized French and Creole as its official languages in its 1804 constitution.

French remained the language of choice in francophone communities left adrift by the loss of the first colonial empire, such as the Quebec and Montreal areas of Canada after 1763. Further south, French colonizers mixed with Native American and African slave groups to form hybrid creole cultures in Louisiana and the South, while French creoles emerged in other parts of the Caribbean and Antilles. Similar creolization occurred in Madagascar and in French enclaves such as Pondicherry in British India.

The global standing of French is bolstered by *l'Organisation internationale de la Francophonie* (the International Organization of French-Speaking Governments), the state-sponsored Institut Français and Alliance Française, and by state-managed radio broadcasters. It has been argued that French may one day displace English as the number one world language, though this is probably due more to wishful thinking than any notable trends. Indeed, a movement is afoot in former French colonies in Africa to switch to English as their first school-taught language.

Soft Power

In the late 2010s, France was recognized as a leading proponent of global soft power. This owes much to its status as the world's most visited tourist destination. Besides the obvious attractions of Paris, the country contains fifty world heritage sites, the third-largest number after Italy and China. Its "gastronomic meal" and "artisanal know-how and culture of baguette bread" are listed on UNESCO's Representative List of the Intangible Cultural Heritage of Humanity—an apt reminder of the perennial global reach and prestige of French cuisine.

A Coca-Cola advertisement in the Atlas mountains: American and French cultural influences vie with each other in countries such as Morocco.

France's biggest rival in the soft power leagues remains the United States. From resentment at postwar "Coca-Colonization" to later attacks on neo-liberalism, denigration of American culture has long been an essential element of modern French life. Paradoxically, this antipathy is mingled with intense and sometimes uncritical admiration. Despite France's well-deserved reputation for filmmaking, for example, box-office receipts show much higher admissions figures for Hollywood films. French consumer culture has always had a strong American flavor.

Anti-Americanism has taken on new colors in the era of globalization, which is widely seen as serving US commercial interests at the expense of French political traditions. Whereas once the Communists led hostility toward the US, now the far right carries the banner. Yet anti-American sentiment still pervades the political mainstream in debates over French autonomy and national identity, with splenetic flurries over the use of the English language and of *franglais*. These outbursts are diminishing, however, for the *Académie française* seems aware that it is fighting a losing battle in defense of "pure" French. The English language has a bigger place in French cultural life than ever before.

Buzzwords of the Culture Wars

The memory wars that began in the 1970s have not expunged xenophobia or antisemitism from French political life. If anything, both have grown stronger in the intervening decades. Jean-Marie Le Pen's comment in 1987 that the gas chambers were a "mere detail" in the history of World War II was a reminder of the far right's enduring anti-Jewish sentiment, but in practice the National Front has trained its sights on immigrants from the Arab world, mainly those from former North African colonies.

Other right-leaning parties have tried to make electoral hay from immigration. From 1986 to 1993, the conservative minister of the interior, Charles Pasqua, passed a series of tough laws making immigration of family members more difficult and easing the deportation of those without legal rights to stay. A left-wing protest against the Pasqua Laws that brought the *SOS Racisme* movement to the fore was accompanied by demonstrations in solidarity with *sans papiers* (undocumented immigrants).

Yet hostility to outsiders seems increasingly hardwired into parts of French mainstream political culture.

In 1968, roughly 6.5 percent of France's population was born in another country. In 2021, that figure stood at 10 percent. Most of the immigrants in the 1960s were from southern Europe. The official collection of data on ethnicity was prohibited in 1978, on the grounds that it replicated racial and antisemitic profiling under Vichy. This makes generalization necessarily vague, but it seems likely that anywhere from three to five million are Muslims, many from the former colonies of North Africa, especially Algeria, Morocco, and Tunisia. It is these and other new African arrivals who are the principal targets of anti-immigrant rhetoric, much of which revolves around the notion of laïcité, or secularism.

Laïcité

Laïcité entered dictionaries in the late nineteenth century. It denoted the idea that the national schooling system should be a level playing field where civic values could be inculcated in young citizens without interference from organized religion. The notion can be traced back to Voltaire's famous anticlerical call to *écrasez l'infâme!* Rarely heard in political debate from 1914 onward, the term laïcité began to appear again in the 1990s. Whereas a century beforehand the word was mainly directed at Catholicism, it was now Islam that was in the crosshairs.

The far right has proved adept at equating any supposed failure of Muslims to conform with "republican" ideas of integration into French culture with the rise of militant and fundamentalist Islam in the wider world. The 1989 fatwa against British writer Salman

Rushdie's *The Satanic Verses* made a big impact in France. Anxieties were further amplified by the Gulf War of 1990–1991, the 9/11 attacks in the United States (2001), and the Iraq War (2003). Bombings by militant Islamists in the Saint-Michel subway station in Paris in 1995 and other security incidents since have given the larger conflicts in the Middle East powerful domestic urgency.

In the immediate aftermath of the 1989 headscarf affair, decisions on whether Muslim dress should be allowed in schools were initially left to schoolteachers. Pressure from far-right groups forced the topic onto the national stage, especially under the presidency of the right-wing former mayor of Paris, Jacques Chirac. From 2004, a national ban was instituted on "ostentatious" signs of religious affiliation. In 2011, this was extended to all such markers. Local disputes arose over whether parents wearing headscarves should even be allowed on school premises.

The mainstream right was solidly behind the ban, but it divided the left. Many feminists took a tough pro-laïcité line, viewing the hijab and other Muslim attire as marks of patriarchal domination of women. Their arguments helped legitimate a law in 2010 prohibiting the wearing of face-covering outfits such as the burka and niqab in any public place. A media flurry in 2017 over so-called burkinis at the beach was a reminder that the issue remained alive and deeply contentious.

Black-Blanc-Beur

The success of the famous "Black, White, Arab" soccer squad, which won the World Cup in France in 1998 before going on to triumph in the 2000 European Cup, provided a happy interlude in an almost unrelenting public assault on immigration. Zinedine Zidane, the captain and charismatic star of the squad, was the son of Algerian immigrants, brought up in the tough suburbs of Marseille. But he was largely viewed as an exception rather than the rule.

Banlieue must rival "laïcité" as the buzzword of the modern era. Over the past century, the population of central Paris has fallen by a third to a little over two million. Meanwhile the wider agglomeration around the city has swollen to nearly eleven million—about one-sixth of France's total population in 2020. This suburbanization is typical of most French cities, as the gentrification of city centers has driven out working-class families toward the urban periphery.

The initial model for dealing with these urban emigrants was to house them in *grands ensembles,* housing projects composed of tower blocks built from the late 1950s onward. On the periphery of Paris, new towns—Évry, Cergy, Marne-la-Vallée, and others—were created to absorb families from the inner cities as well as newcomers from the countryside and abroad. The alienating effect of these somewhat soulless semi-urban projects was worsened by wear and tear, a lack of amenities and care, and the sheer number of new arrivals.

In the late twentieth century, rising unemployment hit the suburbs exceptionally hard. Joblessness in the banlieues far exceeded the national average, especially among the young. Petty crime and gang violence swelled as unemployment rates reached 30 or even 40 percent in some places. From 1996, the government invested in urban renewal in areas categorized as *ZUS* (*zones urbaines sensibles*: "Sensitive Urban Areas"). But the problem remained.

Hatred in the Banlieues

The mood of the banlieues was brilliantly captured on film by Matthieu Kassovitz's hard-hitting *La Haine* ("Hatred"), which won the Palme d'Or at the 1996 Cannes film festival. The film depicted the Parisian suburb of Chanteloup-les-Vignes (a *ZUS*, in fact) as a dispiriting, poverty-wracked environment in which the three young protagonists—a Jew, a North African Muslim, and a West African—lived a precarious life of ennui and petty criminality amid constant police harassment. The soundtrack to the film was curated by banlieue-based rappers. French hip-hop and rap have been closely associated with the banlieues since the 1980s, when the Senegalese rapper MC Solaar achieved breakthrough status. France is the second-largest hip-hop market in the world after the United States and the music has a huge following across the francophone world, particularly in French

Canada and West Africa. Rap lyrics have helped spread the use of the verlan argot, a kind of demotic back-slang popular among immigrant communities—as in the *beur* (Arabe) of *black, blanc, beur*.

The bitter social frustration expressed by French hip-hop has sporadically boiled over into collective acts of violence. The anger rose a notch in 2005, when the death of two youngsters chased by the police into an electricity substation in the Paris suburb of Clichy-sous-Bois led to three weeks of rioting across the country. Overall, riots broke out in more than three hundred places, causing extensive damage to hundreds of properties, with numerous vehicle-burnings and some loss of life. The dismissal of the rioters as *racaille* (scum, or riff-raff) by Interior Minister Nicolas Sarkozy was not intended to pacify emotions. Nor was the battery of knee-jerk anti-immigrant measures that followed.

Given the context, Sarkozy's contribution to the memory wars was unhelpful in the extreme: a 2005 law recognizing the contribution French colonists made to French history. The new *loi mémorielle*'s praise for the positive values of colonialism—a sop to *pieds-noirs* voters drawn to the National Front—aroused widespread indignation. The wording was withdrawn the following year. In 2017, French presidential hopeful Emmanuel Macron declared the French colonization of Algeria a crime against humanity. But if he imagined he was putting an end to past controversy, he was wrong.

Urban violence took on darker overtones in 2015 with the assassination in January of journalists from the scandalously irreverent satirical periodical *Charlie Hebdo*. Then the Bataclan music venue attacks in November that year left over a hundred young people dead. The violence was all the more shocking for being conducted not by foreign terrorists but for the most part by radicalized French and Belgian citizens. The incidents stimulated further far-right ire against immigrants and sent shock waves around the world, as evidenced by massive demonstrations of support for the victims.

Voltaire et Charlie

A memorial event for the victims of the 2015 attacks in Paris, on January 11, 2016, brought together a million and a half people around the Place de la République. The mass show of sympathy also proclaimed the principle of free speech pioneered by France during the Enlightenment. There was a sudden frenzied demand for reprints of Voltaire's *Treatise on Tolerance* (1763). Across the centuries, the shadow of Voltaire seemed to be showing solidarity with the murdered journalists by proclaiming *Je suis Charlie* ("I am Charlie").

Identity in an Age of Uncertainty

The soul-searching that followed the Paris attacks tapped into a deep undercurrent of nostalgia that had been running beneath

French cultural life since the 1970s. The *Trente Glorieuses* had scarcely drawn to a close when Alain Peyrefitte's bestselling 1975 social critique *Le Mal français* ("The French Malady") ushered in a navel-gazing genre that became widespread in the years that followed. Laments for a golden age of economic growth and social progress ranged from politics and industry to France's diminished place within the world's literature, philosophy, and culture. "Declinism" saw authors of all political persuasions variously bemoaning "the French shipwreck," France's "inexorable decline," "the defeat of French thought," "the fall of France," "the crepuscule of French culture," and so on.

Critics accused the French state of renouncing its great power status by abandoning its historic role as a defender of national interest and identity, both at home and abroad. They were particularly agitated by what they saw as the state's willingness to give in to sectional interest groups. French republicanism, it was declared, should be impervious to any form of *communautarisme*.

Coined in the 1980s but only entering common usage more recently, the word *communautarisme* denotes what in anglophone countries might be called multiculturalism or identity politics. From the mid 2010s, it has been closely associated with the idea of "wokeness" (*le wokisme*). In its original American context, "being woke" signified vigilance over issues of social justice and inequality. But in France—as in Britain—wokeness became a term of denigration for any supposed self-righteous do-goodism. *Le wokisme*, critics felt, camouflaged sectional interests and threatened freedom of expression and equality.

Policies prioritizing education in poorer, ethnically diverse neighborhoods were fiercely attacked on *communautariste* grounds. The same was true of gay rights activism. Civil partnerships (PACS: *pactes civils de solidarité*) were instituted in 1999 and same-sex marriage was legalized in 2013, but to high levels of *anti-communautariste* indignation. LGBTQ individuals still routinely face discrimination in areas such as housing, employment, and access to new reproductive technologies.

As these examples suggest, *anti-communautarisme* spread rapidly from politics and culture to biology and sexuality. Women's rights felt the blast. The so-called *parité* law of 2000 stipulated that political parties had to include 50 percent women on their electoral lists. Yet despite an initial surge in female representation, women continued to lag far behind men in terms of pay and promotion in politics as in other areas of public life. The #MeToo movement from 2017, which in France passed under the name of *#BalanceTonPorc* ("Out Your Pig"), garnered popular support at first. But it soon became a target of right-wing criticism and a public backlash led by celebrities such as the former film icon Catherine Deneuve.

"The Enemy Within"

Distrust of personal identity politics and multiculturalism bled into wider concerns over national identity. The charge of *communautarisme* was leveled against the Muslim community in ways that amplified the 1989 headscarf controversy. In the name of the hallowed republican principle of laïcité (secularism), *communautarisme* became a weapon used to block anything that resembled special treatment for Muslims. Far-right ideologues conflated Islam with Islamism, arguing that religious fundamentalism was sweeping the French nation. Marine Le Pen, whose takeover of the leadership of the National Front from her father in 2011 was supposed to detoxify the brand, compared

Muslims praying on public streets with the state of cities under Nazi occupation.

Throughout the 2010s, the populist journalist and broadcaster Eric Zemmour raised the stakes even higher with outrageous attacks on the "enemy within." His own take on declinism, the widely read book *Le Suicide français* (2014), lambasted the country's elites for following a "feminist, pro-gay, egalitarian identity agenda" that was bringing the country to its knees. He berated the May '68 generation and breathtakingly defended the record of Vichy and Pétain regarding the Jews.

In 2021, Zemmour fully embraced the Great Replacement conspiracy theory espoused by the far-right thinker Renaud Camus, which holds that a plot is afoot to replace the indigenous French people with intolerant Muslims. Authentic France, he argued, had been rendered fragile by decadence and decay and was in danger of collapse under the "Islamist" menace. Zemmour's campaign for president went down in flames in 2022. Yet white supremacism had openly returned to French politics, and the center of gravity of public debate had been nudged ever further to the right.

The Price of Austerity

The state already stood accused of surrendering French interests to the "Anglo-Saxon" economic philosophy of neo-liberalism. The Eurozone crisis provoked by the huge banking default of 2008 ramped up criticism of both neo-liberal ideas and the European Union itself. The decade of economic turmoil that ensued saw living standards for the majority of the population plummet.

The French government proved to be less in thrall to laissez-faire capitalism than was often claimed. President Nicolas Sarkozy's early measures to bail out the banks and supply a massive stimulus to hard-hit businesses were, after all, in keeping with the French *dirigiste* tradition. Yet this heavy spending reduced the government's capacity and indeed its will for wider action. Austerity became the new watchword.

The tenures of both the right-of-center Sarkozy from 2007 and the mild and uncharismatic Socialist François Hollande from 2012 were fatally tainted by the fallout from austerity policies. The men differed on any number of policies, but they both embraced budgetary orthodoxy—and paid dearly for it. Unusually for the Fifth Republic, neither man succeeded to a second term. Sarkozy was defeated in the final runoff in 2012, while Hollande withdrew from running again in 2017 when he sensed public opinion turning against him.

The mood of popular discontent was hammered home in a series of wholly unexpected blows to the body politic. The first of these was the victory of a complete outsider in the presidential elections of 2017. Drawn from a banking background, Emmanuel Macron had served as Hollande's economics minister from 2014 to 2016. Spotting a gap provided by the president's unpopularity, he launched his own centrist pro-European party, *La République en Marche*. Voters deserted the Socialists and center-right in droves to put him into the final runoff for the presidency. From that point he was a shoo-in to defeat the National Front's Marine Le Pen, who nevertheless polled more strongly than her father had in 2002. At thirty-nine, Macron was the youngest French head of state since Napoleon.

Macron's election highlighted the depths of disgruntlement felt by the French public toward the conventional party system. This was confirmed in the ensuing 2017 legislative elections. Macron's *En Marche!* ("Forward!") party registered a resounding

The view from abroad: Macron as Napoleon, pictured during a carnival
parade on Rose Monday on February 12, 2018, in Mainz, Germany

victory with nearly 30 percent of the popular vote and a strong
majority in the National Assembly. Centrists suffered, but leftists
even more so, with the Socialists recording their worst performance ever. Although Le Pen's National Front polled strongly, the
voting system left it with only a handful of deputies.

The Macron/*En Marche* victories were just the first of several
seismic shifts in French political life. The second was the so-called
Gilets jaunes ("yellow jackets") episode. Springing up shortly after
the election, this highly unusual grassroots protest movement
was triggered by plans to raise gasoline taxes as part of a broader
ecological strategy. On November 17, 2018, nearly three hundred

thousand demonstrators appeared seemingly out of nowhere wearing the high-visibility fluorescent jackets that all motorists in France are obliged to carry in their vehicles. A favorite tactic was to blockade traffic circles, using social media to mobilize before taking to the streets. Over the next year or so, some fifty thousand *Gilets jaunes* protests and demonstrations occurred across the country.

Who were the Gilets jaunes?

The *Gilets jaunes* formed a movement that was very much sui generis. It was not a youth uprising like 1968. Nor was it the product of the inner city like most major revolts before, nor did it emanate from the troubled banlieues. The participants were instead overwhelmingly white workers who came mainly from rural locations and the suburban peripheries of major towns. Women, notably single mothers, were comparatively overrepresented. Surprisingly few of the activists had existing political or trade union affiliations beforehand and they resisted attempts by all major parties to enlist them afterward. Most protesters belonged to what became known as *le précariat*, employed but living precarious lives on the cusp of destitution.

Social justice, broadly construed, lay at the heart of the *Gilets jaunes* movement. Economic torpor since the 2008 financial meltdown and a decade of austerity had exacerbated inequality. Average wages rose by over 3 percent a year during the *Trente Glorieuses*. Wage growth now dragged along at a mere 1 percent or less. Yet while the average income of 99 percent of the French population had risen by around 25 percent between 1983 and 2015, that of the richest 1 percent had doubled. It seemed that for the very wealthy, the *Trente Glorieuses* had never ended.

President of the Rich

Macron showed few signs of being the providential leader that some of his followers had imagined. More cerebral than charismatic, he clearly lacked the common touch and appeared arrogant and oblivious to social needs. Yet the breadth of the *Gilets jaunes* protests and the scale of public support they attracted spurred the "President of the Rich" to action, offering a package of reforms, price freezes, and the like on a scale that no political party or union had secured for decades. The plan seemed to do the trick. The protest movement soon petered out, its days of action degenerating into vandalism in city centers to which far-right thugs contributed their efforts.

Voters dealt a further blow to the political establishment in 2022. Although turnout was over 70 percent for the presidential elections, for the first time ever it fell below 50 percent in the legislative races. Indeed, the figure had been falling since the 1990s. Coming hard on the heels of the *Gilets jaunes* protests, the dire showing suggested there was an alarming disconnect between social demands and the political parties who claimed to represent the public.

In 2022, Macron's main contender for the presidency was Marine Le Pen, who had herself fought off a far-right challenge from the nativist *Reconquête* ("Reconquest") party of Eric Zemmour. The presidential runoff with Macron was closer than in 2017. But the real progress of the far right was felt in the ensuing legislative elections. Though Macron's renamed Renaissance Party still emerged as the largest group, it failed to secure a majority. After building up Macron as the great hope of 2017, voters were now inclined to take him down a peg or two.

By contrast, the *Rassemblement national* (or "National Rally," as the National Front renamed itself) improved both its share of the vote and the number of its deputies—albeit from a very low base. A left-leaning, green coalition, the New Ecological and Social People's Union (*Nouvelle Union populaire écologique et sociale*, or NUPES) fared better and would constitute the main opposition party. But the volatile temperament and erratic views of the ex-Socialist Jean-Luc Mélenchon, who had cobbled the group together, cast doubts on its prospects and longevity.

Taken together, Macron's electoral triumph in 2017, the *Gilets jaunes* phenomenon of 2018, and the surge of the far right in 2022 constituted a devastating assault on France's political establishment. Some features of this change—a growing disenchantment with politics, the weakening of the left, and a shift to populism on the right—aligned with developments elsewhere in Europe and the world. But others were particular to France.

In particular, the patience of lower-income voters was wearing thin. Many blue-collar workers had steered their voting from left to hard left and then far right, but this was often because the places where they worked had suffered from the shakeout caused by globalization. Their long-term voting patterns remained uncertain. Although immigrants and identity politics hogged the headlines, many voters were less obsessed by these issues than the newsmakers. Beneath the media whirligig, economic issues and social class were still important to most people.

Existential Threats

An almost empty Trocadero square as COVID-19 restrictions came into force in March 2020 in Paris

For all its internal troubles, the French economy faced severe pressure from two external shocks, the outbreak of the COVID-19 pandemic and the Russian invasion of Ukraine in 2022. France was one of the European countries hit hardest by the virus. In the two main waves of the pandemic in 2020–2021, the country's health and emergency services—whose quality was well above the international norm—were given a stringent stress test.

Although the government's prompt response buffered the initial blow, the pandemic revealed bureaucratic weaknesses that became even more dangerous once vaccines were identified and produced. The effectiveness of the vaccine roll-out was further dented by widespread popular feeling against the government plan. Vaccination hesitancy was higher than in other European countries. This appears to have been linked less to hostility toward science than to a growing distrust in political elites.

From the start of the pandemic, Macron announced that the two aims of government strategy were to save as many lives as possible and to prevent the economy—including the health sector—from crashing. As was the case globally, it proved hard to juggle these competing objectives. Huge investment was required to keep firms in business and provide support to families. But an over-hasty relaxation of health measures to kick-start the economy led to a resurgence in cases and a second period of confinement.

As the affliction appeared to subside in 2022, overall mortality figures in France were lower than in most comparable countries, while the economy had gingerly embarked on the road to recovery. At that very moment, however, it received another mighty blow from the Russian invasion of Ukraine. France and the rest of the EU offered Ukraine military and financial support. Hostility toward Russia came at a price, however, with the cessation of Russian oil and gas supplies to Western Europe. Energy prices rocketed across the continent and fueled levels of inflation not seen for decades, wrecking any chance of a swift post-COVID recovery.

The Ukraine crisis scrambled the European map, triggering a drift back toward former Cold War attitudes and policies. War also revealed the fragility of France's energy security in ways that demanded determined action. Macron capped energy prices to protect those on low incomes, but this was too costly to be anything more than a short-term measure.

Both COVID and Ukraine helped draw attention to an issue that had been rapidly climbing up the government agenda: the environment. From disease outbreaks to crop shortages, there was no hiding from the global deterioration caused by climate change. The most eye-catching threats to France itself were the successive

"France is a patchwork of migrations": Supporters celebrate the second-round victory of the New Popular Front in central Paris in July 2024.

heatwave years from the 2010s onward, which affected pollution levels and crop yields. To these concerns were added the rising risk of flooding due to extreme rainfall and damage to coastal defenses caused by rising sea levels.

Thankfully, climate change denial remained extremely low in France, with polls suggesting the French were more worried about global warming than most other Europeans. Mounting an effective response to the climate challenge was asking a lot of the wider population, especially given its growing distrust in government. Yet the internationally ratified Paris Agreement of 2015 had set an inspiring lead. Voices calling for "growing back green" after the COVID and Ukraine crises struck a chord in government as well as in the broader society.

Uneasy Lies the Head

The early 2020s saw the French government struggling to deal with with a vast array of multifaceted problems, from disease control and climate change to conflicts in Ukraine and Gaza. Even the relatively minor tinkering of "Macronomics" seemed to antagonize much of the population. Attempts at pension reform in 2023 incurred widespread anger. This was further amplified by the extremely violent police tactics used for crowd control during the public demonstrations that followed.

Macron's decision to force through changes against a recalcitrant legislature gained him a fund of public ill will, along with accusations of currying favor with far-right voters. His attempt to regain popularity by establishing the constitutional right of women to abortion was a significant progressive step—a world first, in fact. But its failure to move the dial in terms of his own popularity was displayed by a disastrous showing in the European elections of early June 2024, in which the far right received an uncomfortably large share of the vote.

Macron's response to this defeat was to go for broke and call snap national legislative elections. The results were hardly inspiring. The National Rally led the first round of voting with 33 percent of the ballot. But the real possibility of the first far-right government since Vichy galvanized the left into preventive action. Socialists, Greens, Communists, and other left-wing groups joined forces under the historically loaded name of the New Popular Front (*Nouveau Front Populaire*).

The electoral campaign was short and bitter. Marine Le Pen had "detoxified" her father's old party to some extent. Neither overt antisemitism nor coded neo-Nazism were on display, while the party nominally accepted gay marriage, women's rights, and the abolition of the death penalty. There was no longer any talk of "Frexit" either. Yet the populist nationalism of the party still expressed itself in rampant xenophobia, a hard line on immigration, and advocacy for "national preference" regarding jobs, welfare, and housing.

The campaign provoked the highest turnout for legislative elections since 1997. At the end of the day, the far right still led the popular vote but fell short of the numbers needed for a majority. Indeed, its parliamentary representation lagged behind the leftist New Popular Front and Macron's new centrist *Ensemble* ("Together") group. The 2024 elections had produced a three-way split in which no party alone could achieve a majority. Unable or unwilling to break the impasse, Macron kicked the can down the road by declaring a truce until after the Olympic Games.

Olympic Truce

Starting a mere two weeks after the elections, the 2024 Olympic and Paralympic Games in Paris seemed to offer a glimmer of redemption for Macron's government. The Games were an epic carnival of soft power, the kind of international event that France could manage supremely well. Despite the virtual closure of the city center for normal business on security grounds, the event allowed Paris to showcase itself in the tradition of the great universal expositions of old.

Laying Down a Legacy

Long before the starting gun was fired, Macron was milking the Games for political and economic gain. Many of the sporting venues were located out in the banlieues as well as within city limits, boosting the economy beyond the *Boulevard Périphérique*. The athletes' village, built in the economically disadvantaged locations of Saint-Denis and Saint-Ouen, constituted a legacy project in terms of housing and infrastructure. As a further gesture of political goodwill, the government worked hard to make the Games the greenest on record, with only half the carbon footprint of previous events and a solid commitment to sustainability and heritage.

For all the pomp and razzle-dazzle of the opening ceremony, deeper troubles within French society crept within the stadium walls. Fresh from hurling abuse at players of foreign heritage in the European Soccer Championship, the far right channeled their ire at the French-Malian singer-songwriter Aya Nakamura, the most streamed music artist in France, after she was tapped to open the Games. At the same time, the government seemed to be borrowing from the far-right playbook by prohibiting its female Muslim athletes from wearing the hijab—the only competing nation to do so. Only months earlier, France had become the first state in history to make abortion a constitutional right. Now laïcité was taking it to some strange and paradoxical places. At the end of the day, France was spared the embarrassment of a far-right government presiding over one of the world's most watched events. And in the end, the success of the Games—with a healthy haul of medals for France— stoked a warm glow among Parisians and visitors alike, while providing a respite from high (and low) politics and everyday woes. "It is possible to be together, and to be happy!" said Mayor Anne Hidalgo, a Socialist, with relief and perhaps some incredulity.

That peace of mind would be sorely tested once the Olympic Truce ended. And yet, as the political cavalcade resumed, there was an Olympic Truce moment for quiet reflection on January 7, 2025, when Hidalgo and Macron laid wreaths at the site of the former offices of Charlie Hebdo. On the tenth anniversary of the attacks, France faced an uncertain future, forced to confront the ghosts of a troubled past while maintaining the openness to the wider world that has made it what it is today: a rich tapestry of people, of ideas, of things; a complex and by turns exasperating and inspiring society that remains a source of boundless fascination.

Zinedine Zidane (left), poster child of a multicultural France, receives the torch at the Olympic opening ceremony in Paris, July 26, 2024.

Further Reading

Robert Aldrich, *Greater France: A History of French Overseas Expansion* (1996)

Dave Andress, ed., *The Routledge Handbook of French History* (2023)

John Ardagh, *The New French Revolution: A Social and Economic Survey of France* (1968)

Edward Berenson, Vincent Duclert, Christophe Prochasson, eds., *The French Republic: History, Values, Debates* (2011)

David A. Bell, *Shadows of Revolution: Reflections on France, Past and Present* (2016)

Joseph Bergin, *A History of France* (2015)

Patrick Boucheron, ed., *France in the World: A New Global History* (2019)

Fernand Braudel, *The Identity of France*, 2 vols. (1986, 1988)

Emil Chabal, *France* (2020)

Alice Conklin et al., *France and its Empire since 1870* (2nd edition, 2014)

William Doyle, *The Oxford History of the French Revolution* (3rd edition, 2018)

Sudhir Hazareesingh, *How the French Think* (2015)

Julian Jackson, *De Gaulle* (2019)

Colin Jones, *The Cambridge Illustrated History of France* (1994)

Gérard Noiriel, *The French Melting-Pot: Immigration, Citizenship and National Identity* (1996)

Jeremy D. Popkin, *A History of Modern France* (5th edition, 2020)

Roger Price, *A Concise History of France* (2nd edition, 2014)

Vanessa Schwartz, *Modern France: A Very Short Introduction* (2011)

Tyler Stovall, *Transnational France: The Modern History of a Universal Nation* (2015)

Henriette Walter, *France Inside Out: The Worldwide Development of the French Language in the Past, the Present and the Future* (1994)

Chris Wickham, *Medieval Europe* (2016)

Ian Wood, *The Merovingian Kingdoms, 450–751* (1994)

Image Credits

p. 82: Monopod or skiapod. Woodcut from Nuremberg Chronicles, 1493. Public domain via Wikimedia Commons.

p. 85: Detail from *Le Massacre de la Saint Barthélemy* (painting) by François Dubois. Musée cantonal des Beaux-Arts, Lausanne, Switzerland. Public domain.

p. 87: Henry IV's equestrian statue on the Pont Neuf, Paris. Engraving. Bibliothèque nationale de France. Public domain.

p. 96: Louis XIV. Bust by Bernini, 1665. Photographer "Louis le Grand" via Wikipedia (CC BY-SA 2.5).

p. 101: Two designs for the east façade of the Louvre: (a) Drawing by Bernini, 1664. Courtauld Gallery/public domain. (b) Louvre colonnade. Final design as built. Copperplate engraving from Blondel's *Architecture françoise*, 1756. Public domain.

p. 103: Sun motif from Versailles. Architectural feature (photograph). Author/credit: Jebulon, available under the Creative Commons CC0 1.0 Universal Public Domain Dedication.

p. 110: Portrait of Voltaire from the workshop of Nicolas de Largilliere, c. 1720. Musée de l'Histoire de France/public domain.

p. 113: Still from *Dangerous Liaisons* (film), 1988 AJ Pics/Alamy Stock Photo © Warner Bros.

p. 117: Rue St Honoré Doll. Public domain. BTEU/RKMLGE/Alamy Stock Photo

p. 124: *Taking of the Bastille* by Jean-Pierre Houdël, 1789. Original painting held by Bibliothèque nationale de France. Public domain, made available by Gallica Digital Library.

p. 128: Guillotine cartoon: "Dialogue," 1793. Public domain. French Revolution Digital Archive, Stanford University/Bibliothèque nationale de France.

p. 130: *Sans-culottes en armes*: character portraits by Jean-Baptiste Lesueur. Public domain. Musée Carnavalet, *Histoire de Paris*, Les Musées de la Ville de Paris.

p. 131: *M. M. J. Robespierre*. Engraving by Gabriel Feisinger after a portrait by Guérin, 1789. Bibliothèque nationale de France/public domain.

p. 137: Napoleon in Egypt. Oil painting by Jean-Léon Gérôme. Princeton University Art Museum/public domain.

p. 141: *The Dying Gaul*. Sculpture attributed to Epigonus, c. 230 BCE. Capitoline Museums, Rome. Public domain. Creative Commons license (CC BY 2.0).

p. 143: *Napoleon Crossing the Alps* by Jacques-Louis David, 1803 (Belvedere version). Österreichische Galerie Belvedere, Vienna, Austria. Public domain via Google Cultural Institute.

p. 147: *Liberty Leading the People* by Eugene Delacroix, 1830 (detail). Louvre, Paris. Public domain.

p. 151: Honoré de Balzac, caricature/cartoon by Jean-Jacques Grandville, c. 1835–1836. Les Musées de la Ville de Paris. Public domain.

p. 155: Boulevard Haussmann in Paris.
Author/credit: Thierry Bézecourt via Wikipedia (CC BY 3.0).

p. 156: Paris commune: *Monument to the Victims of Revolutions* by Paul Moreau-Vauthoer. Photographer: LPLT/Wikimedia Commons

p. 158: Nineteenth-century postcard of Guimard Metro design for Bastille Station, Paris. Reproduction in public domain.

p. 159: A still from *Voyage to the Moon*, 1902. Public domain.

p. 160: Self-portrait by Baudelaire, c. 1844. Bibliothèque des Arts Décoratifs. Public domain.

p. 162: "General View of the Universal Exposition of Nice, 1884." Illustration. INTERFOTO/Alamy Stock Photo

p. 166: Contemporary postcard of Kanak village, Paris Exposition, 1889. Public domain.

p. 171: French Republic postage stamp, c. 1893. Public domain.

p. 174: Spahi cavalry unit near Furnes in Belgium, 1914. Photograph held by Bibliothèque nationale de France. Public domain.

p. 177: Alfred Dreyfus in his cell in Guyana, 1898. After a stereoscopy sold by F. Hamel, Altona-Hambourg, collection Fritz Lachmund. Public domain via Wikimedia.

p. 182: Clemenceau at the National Assembly. Newspaper illustration by J. Simoni, November 11, 1918.

p. 184: Monument to the victims of WWI. Photographer: Rouleau. Public domain via Wikimedia.

p. 186: France's civilizing mission. Poster from 1951 Paris exposition © B. Milleret by permission of GrandPalaisRmn (Musée du Quai Branly - Jacques Chirac)/photographer: Hervé Lewandowski.

p. 189. Josephine Baker receives the medal of the city of Paris, March 3, 1956. Photograph. ZUMA Press, Inc./Alamy Stock Photo

p. 192: *Exposition Internationale des Arts et Techniques dans la Vie Moderne*, Paris, 1937. Credit (editor): La Photolith. Public domain via Wikipedia.

p. 197: French gendarmes registering Jews in Pithiviers, May 1941. Photograph. Credit: *Bundesarchiv Bild*. Image available under Creative Commons license (CC-BY-SA 3.0).

p. 199: Maquisards group photographed in Châteauneuf-de-Bordette, 1944. Public domain.

p. 201: General de Gaulle and entourage, Champs Élysées, Paris, August 26, 1944. Credit: Imperial War Museums. Public domain.

p. 203: Petain on trial, July 1945. Unknown photographer/copyright expired.

p. 205: French woman and British soldier walking through ruins of Caen, July 10, 1944. Photograph. Credit: E. G. Malindine/Imperial War Museums

p. 208: Vietnamese troops plant a flag over captured French headquarters, Dien Bien Phu, 1954. Public domain. Source: Creative Commons/Vietnam People's Army Museum System

p. 213. "Dior dress incident," October 1947. Photograph: Walter Carone/Paris Match archive via Getty Images.

p. 217: HLM/bidonville in Saint-Denis, 1950s. Photograph. French national archives. Public domain.

p. 219: *The Kiss by the Hôtel de Ville* by Robert Doisneau, 1950. Photo by Robert DOISNEAU/Gamma-Rapho via Getty Images

p. 222: Student demonstration at Sorbonne University, Paris, May 1968. Photo by GERARD-AIME/Gamma-Rapho via Getty Images

p. 227: Simone de Beauvoir in a crowd of women, Bobigny abortion trial, 1972. Photograph. Artault Erwan/Sygma via Getty Images.

p. 232: Louvre courtyard with glass pyramid by I. M. Pei. Creative commons © Irene Ledyaeva

p. 235: Maurice Papon at his trial, October 14, 1997. Illustration by court artist. AFP via Getty Images

p. 237: Graffito: *Ici on noié les Algeriens.* Photograph, October 1961. Authors: Claude Angeli and Jean Texier. First published in the French journal *L'Humanité*, 1985. Image made available under fair use license via Wikipedia.

p. 243: Licorne (Unicorn) atomic weapon test, Fangataufa Atoll, July 3, 1970. Photograph. Photo Researchers/Alamy Stock Photo

p. 245: Coca-Cola advertizement in Atlas Mountains, Morocco. Photograph. Photographer: ciukes. Image available via Wikipedia under Creative Commons license (CC BY 2.0).

p. 250: Still from *La Haine*, 1996. Movie still. Moviestore Collection Ltd/Alamy Stock Photo

p. 252: *Je Suis Charlie* poster. Gamma-Rapho Collection via Getty Images. Photographer: Herve Champollion

p. 257: Macron as Napoleon, carnival parade float in Mainz, Germany, February 12, 2018. Photograph. Photo by Andreas Arnold/AFP via Getty Images

p. 261: Empty Trocadero square during COVID-19 outbreak, Paris, March 2020. Photograph: JJZ/Alamy Stock Photo

p. 263: "France is a patchwork of migrations." Demonstrators with banner, central Paris, July 2024. Photograph. Panos Pictures Ltd.

p. 267: Zinedine Zidane receives the Olympic torch from hooded figure, July 26, 2024. Photograph by Baptiste Fernandez Collection. Icon Sport via Getty Images.

Acknowledgments

My warmest thanks go to Ben Yarde-Buller at Old Street Publishing and Anna Bliss at The Experiment for acting as inspiration and guide through the production process. It was a particular pleasure working with them, along with Digby Lidstone and Kieron Connolly (editors), and James Nunn (maps and graphics), as part of the team during the final stages. A simple acknowledgment falls far short of meeting the intellectual debts I have incurred over the course of a lifetime of research on French history; a full listing of friends, colleagues, and individuals encountered and learnt from would risk turning this shortest into the longest history of France. Salut et fraternité to all of them. I draw heavily on the shrewd advice of Catherine Clarke at the Felicity Bryan Agency. And thanks, finally, to my wife, Jo McDonagh, for always being there.

Index

About the Author

COLIN JONES is Emeritus Professor of History at Queen Mary University of London and visiting professor at the University of Chicago. He is a fellow of the British Academy, former president of the Royal Historical Society, and Officier in the *Ordre des Palmes académiques*. He is the author and editor of many works on French history, including *The Cambridge Illustrated History of France*, *The Great Nation: France from Louis XV to Napoleon*, *Paris: Biography of a City* (awarded the Enid MacLeod Prize of the Franco-British Society), *The Smile Revolution in Eighteenth-Century Paris*, *Versailles*, and *The Fall of Robespierre: 24 Hours in Revolutionary Paris*.

Also available in the Shortest History series

Trade Paperback Originals • $16.95 US | $21.95 CAN

978-1-61519-569-5

978-1-61519-820-7

978-1-61519-814-6

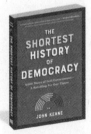

978-1-61519-896-2

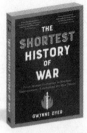

978-1-61519-930-3

978-1-61519-914-3

978-1-61519-948-8

978-1-61519-950-1

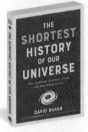

978-1-61519-973-0

978-1-891011-34-4

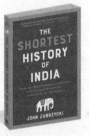

978-1-61519-997-6

978-1-891011-45-0

978-1-891011-66-5

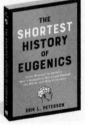

978-1-891011-88-7

979-8-89303-060-0